FLOYD CLYMER'S MOTORCYCLIST'S LIBRARY

BOOK OF THE B.S.A.

A COMPLETE GUIDE FOR OWNERS AND PROSPECTIVE PURCHASERS OF B.S.A. MACHINES

WRITTEN BY AN INDEPENDENT OWNER-DRIVER, DEALING WITH EVERY PHASE OF MOTOR-CYCLING FROM THE REGISTRATION TO SELLING OF THE MACHINE SECOND-HAND, INCLUDING CHAPTERS ON DRIVING, TOURING, LEGAL MATTERS, INSURANCE, OVERHAULING

BY

"WAYSIDER"

(F. J. Camm)

FOURTH EDITION
1930

ANNOUNCEMENT

By special arrangement with the original publishers of this book, Sir Isaac Pitman & Son, Ltd., of London, England, we have secured the exclusive publishing rights for this book, as well as all others in THE MOTORCYCLIST'S LIBRARY.

Included in THE MOTORCYCLIST'S LIBRARY are complete instruction manuals covering the care and operation of respective motorcycles and engines; valuable data on speed tuning, and thrilling accounts of motorcycle race events. See listing of available titles elsewhere in this edition.

We consider it a privilege to be able to offer so many fine titles to our customers.

FLOYD CLYMER
Publisher of Books Pertaining to Automobiles and Motorcycles
2125 W. PICO ST.   LOS ANGELES 6, CALIF.

INTRODUCTION

Welcome to the world of digital publishing ~ the book you now hold in your hand, while unchanged from the original edition, was printed using the latest state of the art digital technology. The advent of print-on-demand has forever changed the publishing process, never has information been so accessible and it is our hope that this book serves your informational needs for years to come. If this is your first exposure to digital publishing, we hope that you are pleased with the results. Many more titles of interest to the classic automobile and motorcycle enthusiast, collector and restorer are available via our website at www.VelocePress.com. We hope that you find this title as interesting as we do.

NOTE FROM THE PUBLISHER

The information presented is true and complete to the best of our knowledge. All recommendations are made without any guarantees on the part of the author or the publisher, who also disclaim all liability incurred with the use of this information.

TRADEMARKS

We recognize that some words, model names and designations, for example, mentioned herein are the property of the trademark holder. We use them for identification purposes only. This is not an official publication.

INFORMATION ON THE USE OF THIS PUBLICATION

This manual is an invaluable resource for the classic motorcycle enthusiast and a "must have" for owners interested in performing their own maintenance. However, in today's information age we are constantly subject to changes in common practice, new technology, availability of improved materials and increased awareness of chemical toxicity. As such, it is advised that the user consult with an experienced professional prior to undertaking any procedure described herein. While every care has been taken to ensure correctness of information, it is obviously not possible to guarantee complete freedom from errors or omissions or to accept liability arising from such errors or omissions. Therefore, any individual that uses the information contained within, or elects to perform or participate in do-it-yourself repairs or modifications acknowledges that there is a risk factor involved and that the publisher or its associates cannot be held responsible for personal injury or property damage resulting from the use of the information or the outcome of such procedures.

WARNING!

One final word of advice, this publication is intended to be used as a reference guide, and when in doubt the reader should consult with a qualified technician.

PREFACE

OUTSTANDING changes in B.S.A. design include a forged steel backbone incorporated in the recently introduced duplex cradle construction of the frame, the adoption of sump lubrication on most four-stroke models, the fitting of taper roller bearings to front and rear hubs, the fitting of hinged rear mudguards and spring-up stands, the fitting of shock absorbers (in most cases of the hand adjusted type) on all models, and the introduction of many new features in the design of the engine. The most noteworthy introduction to the present series of machines is, of course, the three wheeler with front wheel drive, which the reader will find fully described in this book. The changes mentioned above have necessitated a complete revision of many of the chapters in this book and the inclusion of a considerable amount of new matter, but I have been inspired in the task by the successes which have attended the previous editions, and I hereby set on record my thanks to the many hundreds of readers who have shown their appreciation in the form of letters, many of which have contained helpful suggestions. I am gratified to know that I have been able to help many readers who have written to me for advice when their mount has not been functioning as the makers intended it should, and I would repeat that I hope all readers of this volume will write to me when they are in difficulty or in need of advice regarding B.S.A. Motor-cycles. In most cases I am able to reply by return of post.

"WAYSIDER."

PREFACE TO THIRD EDITION

NOTEWORTHY introductions to the B.S.A. range, since the last edition of this book went to press, are the 1·74 h.p. two-stroke model and the 4·93 O.H.V. model. Wired-on tyres and internal expanding brakes are now fitted to all models, the round tank 2·49 h.p. two-speed machine has been superseded by the 2·49 De Luxe three-speed model, with taper rectangular-section tank ; all saddles, excluding the two-stroke, now have fore and aft adjustment, a new type of mechanical pump is fitted, frames have been strengthened (particularly at the head), silencers have been increased in capacity—these represent latest developments. Accordingly, much of the matter appearing in earlier editions has necessarily been revised and largely rewritten in this. I thank my readers for the generous reception they have accorded earlier editions.

" WAYSIDER."

" Waysider " writes every month in the *Motor Cyclist Review*.

CONTENTS

CHAP.		PAGE
	PREFACE	
I.	THE VARIOUS B.S.A. MOUNTS	1
II.	REGISTRATION, DRIVING LICENCE AND EQUIPMENT	20
III.	DRIVING	29
IV.	HOW THE ENGINE WORKS	47
V.	MECHANICAL DETAILS OF THE B.S.A.	60
VI.	OVERHAULING	92
VII.	TOURING	112
VIII.	FAULTS : THEIR LOCATION AND REMEDY	119
IX.	LEGAL MATTERS	129
X.	BUYING AND SELLING AN OLD MOUNT	132
XI.	USEFUL INFORMATION	135
	INDEX	143

BOOK OF THE B.S.A.

CHAPTER I

THE VARIOUS B.S.A. MOUNTS

SEVENTEEN B.S.A. motor-cycles are now marketed, ranging from 1·74 h.p. to 9·86 h.p.—one 1·74 h.p. (two-stroke), two 2·49 h.p., three 3·49 h.p., six 4·93 h.p., two 5·57 h.p., one 7·70 h.p., (V-twin), and two 9·86 h.p. (V-twins). The latest addition to the range is the B.S.A. three-wheeler car, which has an air-cooled engine of 9 h.p. (1021 c.c.), and is fully dealt with at the end of this chapter.

Of the seventeen motor-cycles, eight are really de luxe editions, differing only in regarding to brakes, saddles, forks, tyres, gear ratios, or (in one or two cases) type of engine. This leaves nine main models, and in the following seventeen specifications I have given full details of those nine, with only the main points of difference in the specifications of the remaining eight models.

I have presented the specifications in the order of their capacity, with the one exception of the L30-11 model which, having a specification similar in the main to the S30-13 model, follows the specification of the latter.

I would particularly refer the reader to the tables on pages 18 and 19, which contain in a form convenient for quick reference the performance and other data necessary for checking results.

B.S.A. Tank Colours. Those models which are normally fitted with the standard B.S.A. Green Tank can be supplied with a B.S.A. Royal Blue, B.S.A. Maroon, or nickel-plated tank at an extra charge of £1. Those models to which chromium or nickel-plated tanks with top panels in green are fitted as standard can be supplied with tanks plated all over (i.e. without coloured top panels) or with tanks in B.S.A. Green, B.S.A. Royal Blue, or B.S.A. Maroon, at the same price.

Whatever colours are used, all B.S.A. tanks embody the same panelling with the letters B.S.A. as in the past.

The 1·74 h.p. 3-speed Two-stroke Model. ENGINE. Single cylinder, 1·74 h.p. two-stroke, 60 × 61·5 mm. bore and stroke. Aluminium alloy piston. Roller bearing big end. Engine mainshaft mounted on two ball bearings. Large exhaust pipe and silencer mounted on chainstay. Petroil lubrication. Kick-starter engaging direct with engine shaft. Air cleaner fitted to carburettor. Magneto gear driven and mounted behind cylinder.

TRANSMISSION. Enclosed gear drive from engine to layshaft, running in oil. Final drive by roller chain ½ in. pitch by ·305 in., protected by guard. The clutch is mounted on the layshaft, and is of the floating dry plate type controlled by a lever on the left-hand side of the handlebar, with a large diameter cable. The B.S.A. three-speed gear-box in unit construction with the engine is fitted. This is of the constant mesh type, the gear change being effected by dogs. The layshaft is mounted on two ball bearings.

FIG. 1. THE 1·74 H.P. TWO-STROKE MODEL A30-2

The change speed lever is on the right-hand side of the tank. The gear ratios are, 6·8, 10·3 and 14 to 1.

FRAME. Duplex type, designed to give a low riding position and low centre of gravity. It is built up of steel tubes reinforced, trapped and bolted at the ends to eliminate brazed joints. The rear stand is of the kick-up type. Special B.S.A. spring forks with tension spring and shock absorbers, and touring handlebars of the adjustable type are fitted. The saddle tank is supported by brackets on the frame, the capacity being 1¾ gal. New pattern B.S.A. adjustable knee grips are provided. Tyres are 24 in × 2·375 in., on 19 in. × 2¼ in. rims. Both brakes, which are 5½ in. in diameter, are quickly adjustable. Grease gun lubrication to all frame parts.

EQUIPMENT. Spring seat saddle; carrier; complete set of tools in a neat leather roll; inflator.

The 2·49 h.p. O.H.V. Model. Single cylinder engine, 2·49 h.p.,

THE VARIOUS B.S.A. MOUNTS

63 × 80 mm. bore and stroke. Detachable head with large overhead valves mounted at 90°. Enclosed push rods and rocker gear. Forged steel flywheels. Double row roller big-end bearings. Engine mainshaft driving side mounted on ball bearing, plain bearing on gear side. Timing gear specially designed for silent operation. Two 1⅝ in. diameter exhaust pipes, with silencers and fish-tails.

LUBRICATION. Oil sump integral with crankcase, capacity 2½ pints. Gear type pump, driven by skew gearing from mainshaft with the output control accessible from the saddle. The

FIG. 2. THE 2·49 H.P. O.H.V. MODEL

control is on the delivery side of the pump. Oil is supplied to the mainshaft and big-end bearings through special oilways. Visible tell-tale on the timing cover. Surplus oil in the crankcase is returned to the sump by scraper acting on the flywheels. Oil level indicator fitted to filler plug. Automatic variable oil feed to primary chain.

TRANSMISSION. Front and rear chains, ½ in. × ·305 in. Front chain enclosed and lubricated from the engine. The rear chain is protected by a guard. Cam-faced cush drive on engine shaft. The clutch is contained in the large chain wheel, with quick adjustment, and is of the floating dry plate type, controlled by a lever on the left-hand side of the handlebar, with a large diameter cable. A B.S.A. three-speed gear-box is fitted, with kick-starter mechanism enclosed. All gears are constantly in mesh. Change speed lever with gate is mounted on the right-hand side of the tank. Screw adjustment of gear-box position for accurately setting the chain tension. Gear ratios: 6·2, 9·3, and 13·6 to 1.

FRAME. Of new Duplex cradle type. Large diameter top tube and front down tubes brazed in steel head lug. Tubular steel chainstays. B.S.A. new wide type of spring fork with barrel compression spring, and large quickly adjustable shock absorbers. Semi-sporting handlebars, adjustable and reversible for touring or sports position. Chromium-plated, saddle petrol tank with top panel in B.S.A. green; capacity 1¾ gal. New pattern B.S.A. adjustable knee grips. Tyres, 25 in. × 3 in. wired-on type, mounted on heavy guage 19 in. × 2¼ in. rims. Taper roller bearings for hubs. Both brakes are 5½ in. diameter, and of the

FIG. 3. THE 2·49 H.P. MODEL
This illustration also applies to the 3·49 h.p. Model L30-5

internal expanding type, provided with quick adjustment. Front brake operated by lever on the right-hand side of the handlebar, and the rear by toe pedal on the right-hand side of the machine. A rear spring-up stand is fitted, while the front stand is rigidly secured to the guard.

EQUIPMENT. Spring seat saddle, with special fixing, giving low position with fore and aft adjustment; tool-box of increased capacity fitted to chainstays; complete set of tools, including valve spring extractor and grease gun. Inflator is fitted beneath the tank.

FINISH. Chromium plating to petrol tank, silencing system, handlebar and fittings, gear lever and quadrant.

The 2·49 h.p. Model. The specification of this machine is similar to the B30-4 model, except that the engine is 249 c.c. side valve, 63 × 80 mm. bore and stroke; the clutch is of the smaller type; the tank is finished in B.S.A. green, with the usual transfer.

THE VARIOUS B.S.A. MOUNTS

The 3·49 h.p. Model. This machine, which is now designed for solo work only, embodies the same frame and crankcase as model B30-3, but it gives an improved performance. The specification is similar to the B30-3 model, except that the engine is 3·49 h.p., 72 × 85½ mm. bore and stroke; the clutch is the same as that used on the B30-4 model, and the gear ratios are 5·6, 8·2, and 12·1 to 1.

The 3·49 h.p. Model. This machine is designed for light sidecar or commercial work only, and it is not intended as a solo

FIG. 4. THE 4·93 H.P. O.V.H. LIGHT MODEL, S30-19

machine. Its specification is similar to model L30-5 except that the frame is specially reinforced for sidecar work, with integral sidecar lugs and a steering damper fitted. The tyres (26 in. × 3·25 in.) are mounted on heavy gauge 19 in. × 2¼ in. rims; the front mudguard is of the valanced type, whilst the rear is hinged. A lifting handle is also provided to raise the machine on to the rear stand. The gear ratios are 6·6, 9·8, and 14·5 to 1.

The 4·93 O.H.V. Light Model. ENGINE. Single cylinder, 4·93 h.p., 80 × 98 mm. bore and stroke. Detachable head with large overhead valves, mounted at 90°, with enclosed push rods. The rockers are mounted on roller bearings and provided with return springs. Silent timing gear with flat base tappets on wide cams. Mainshaft mounted on ball bearings. Aluminium alloy piston. Two silencers, with fish-tails, mounted on chainstays.

LUBRICATION. Gravity feed to mechanical pump, then to sight feed on timing case, and feeding direct to big-end bearing. Oil control valve on sight feed. Hand pump feeding to crankcase.

The oil is supplied to the primary chain by depressing spring by-pass valve on sight feed. The hubs, fork links, etc., are fitted with grease-gun nipples. An auxiliary oil tank with pedal-operated force feed pump mounted on the seat tube and feeding oil direct to the cylinder wall can be fitted to magneto models at an extra charge.

TRANSMISSION. The front chain $\frac{1}{2}$ in. × ·305 in. is totally enclosed in a two-part chain case. The rear chain $\frac{5}{8}$ in. × $\frac{3}{8}$ in. is protected by a guard. Cam-faced cush drive on engine shaft. The clutch is contained in the large chain wheel, with quick adjustment, and is of the floating dry plate indestructible type, controlled by a lever on the left-hand side of the handlebar. The B.S.A. three-speed gear-box with screw adjustment for front chain tension is fitted. The kick-starter mechanism is enclosed in the gear-box, and the spindle increased in diameter. An inclined gear lever is fitted on the right-hand side of the tank. The gear ratios are: solo, 4·8, 6·6, and 11·4 to 1; sidecar, 5·6, 7·6, and 13·2 to 1.

FRAME. This is designed to give a low riding position, with weldless steel tubing and forged steel lugs throughout. The head lug is of the continuous type, giving great strength, and is fitted with special integral lugs to take B.S.A. sidecars. The head is fitted with a B.S.A. steering damper. Reversible handlebar mounted behind the steering head. The saddle tank is nickel-plated, with the top panel in B.S.A. green; capacity, petrol 2 gal.; oil $3\frac{1}{4}$ pints. New pattern B.S.A. adjustable knee-grips. Tyres, 26 in. × 3 in., mounted on heavy gauge 20 in. × $2\frac{1}{4}$ in. rims. The brakes can be quickly adjusted; the front $5\frac{1}{2}$ in. diameter; the rear 7 in. diameter. The brake cams are increased in width. The front mudguard is made with flared side wings, and the rear guard is hinged to allow of easy removal of the wheel in conjunction with the new low-lift spring-up stand.

EQUIPMENT. Spring seat saddle; tool-box of increased capacity and improved in appearance to conform to the lines of the machine. Complete set of tools, including valve spring extractor; inflator.

The 4·93 h.p. Light Model. This machine has a similar specification to the S30-19 O.H.V. light model, except that the engine is 493 c.c. side valve; the clutch is of a lighter type; the rear chain is $\frac{5}{8}$ in. × $\frac{1}{4}$ in.; and a detachable carrier is included in the specification. The tank is finished in B.S.A. green, with the usual transfer. The oil is delivered from the sight-feed to the crankcase, and an auxiliary oil tank cannot be supplied. The gear ratios are: solo, 5·0, 6·8, 11·8; sidecar, 5·7, 7·8, and 13·5 to 1.

The 4·93 h.p. O.H.V. De Luxe Model. ENGINE. Inclined single

THE VARIOUS B.S.A. MOUNTS

cylinder, 4·93 h.p., 80 × 98 mm. bore and stroke. Detachable head with large overhead valves, mounted at 90° and enclosed push rods. Return springs to rockers and push rods. Silent timing gear with flat base tappets and wide cams driven separately from the crankshaft. Steel flywheels with shafts running on generous ball and roller-bearings. Double row roller big-end bearing fed with oil direct from the mechanical pump.

LUBRICATION. Oil sump integral with crankcase; capacity 3 pints. Submerged gear pump with accessible control knob. Oil supplied direct to the big end. Visible tell-tale on timing

FIG. 5. THE 4·93 H.P. LIGHT MODEL

cover. Surplus oil in the crankcase is returned to the sump by scraper acting on the flywheels. Quick release oil level indicator of dipper type.

TRANSMISSION. Front chain ½ in. × ·305 in., is totally enclosed and lubricated from the engine. The rear chain ⅝ in. × ⅜ in. is protected by a guard. Cam-faced cush drive on engine shaft. The clutch is contained in the large chain wheel, with quick adjustment, and is of the floating dry plate type, controlled by a lever on the left-hand side of the handlebar. The B.S.A. three-speed gear-box is fitted with pivot mounting for chain adjustment. The kick-starter mechanism is enclosed in the gear-box, and the spindle is of larger diameter. An inclined gear lever is fitted on the right-hand side of the tank. The gear ratios are: solo, 4·8, 6·6, and 11·4 to 1; sidecar, 5·6, 7·6, and 13·2 to 1.

FRAME. Of new design, having immense strength without excessive weight. The top member is a single high-tensile steel forging with integral head and seat lugs. Weldless steel tubing for the remainder of the frame is used. Duplex front down tubes terminate in steel forgings, which are bolted to registers on the top frame member; duplex seat tubes thrown further forward to accommodate the battery under the saddle. B.S.A. spring forks with quickly adjustable shock absorbers of increased size. The head is fitted with a B.S.A. steering damper, and integral lugs for sidecar attachment. Reversible handlebar mounted behind the steering head. The saddle tank is chromium plated, with the top panel in B.S.A. green, for fuel only: capacity, $2\frac{1}{4}$ gal. New pattern B.S.A. adjustable knee-grips. Tyres, 26 in. × 3·25 in., mounted on heavy gauge 19 in. × $2\frac{1}{2}$ in. rims. Both brakes are 7 in. diameter and are quickly adjustable. The brake cams are increased in width. The front mudguard is made with flared side wings, and the rear guard is hinged to allow easy removal of the wheel in conjunction with the new low-lift spring-up stand.

EQUIPMENT. De luxe type spring seat saddle; tool-box of increased capacity and improved in appearance to conform to the lines of the machine. Complete set of tools, including valve spring extractor; inflator.

FINISH. Chromium plating to the petrol tank, silencing system, handlebar and fittings, gear lever and quadrant, and engine tappet tubes, etc.

The 3·49 h.p. O.H.V. Model. This machine has a similar specification to model S30-13 O.H.V. de luxe, except that the engine is 3·49 h.p. 72 × $85\frac{1}{2}$ mm. bore and stroke; the push rods are enclosed in plain tubes without return springs; the front brake is $5\frac{1}{2}$ in. diameter; the front fork is of the new design to suit the $5\frac{1}{2}$ in. brake; the saddle is the standard spring seat; the clutch to suit smaller engine; rear chain $\frac{5}{8}$ in. × $\frac{1}{4}$ in.; tyres, 26 in. × 3 in.; gear ratios: solo, 5·7, 7·8, and 13·5 to 1; sidecar, 6·0, 8·2, and 14·3 to 1.

The 4·93 h.p. O.H.V. Model. This is a lighter model than the 4·93 h.p. S30-13 O.H.V. de luxe, but is similar in specification. The following are the main points of difference: The tank is finished in B.S.A. green, with the usual transfer; the front fork is of the new design to suit the $5\frac{1}{2}$ in. front brake; the saddle is the standard spring seat; the push rods are enclosed in plain tubes without return springs; all the bright parts are nickel-plated; and the tyres are 26 in. × 3 in.

The 4.93 h.p. de Luxe Model. ENGINE. Inclined single cylinder side valve, 4·93 h.p., 80 × 98 mm. bore and stroke. The valves are protected by an aluminium cover. Silent timing gear with flat base tappets and wide cams driven separately from the crank-

THE VARIOUS B.S.A. MOUNTS

shaft. The mainshafts are mounted on generous ball and roller bearings. Double row roller big-end bearing fed with oil direct from the mechanical pump. A cylinder priming device for easy starting is fitted.

LUBRICATION. Oil sump integral with crankcase, capacity 3 pints. Submerged gear pump with accessible control knob. Oil supplied direct to the big-end. Visible tell-tale on timing cover. Surplus oil in the crankcase returned to the sump by

FIG. 6. THE 3·49 H.P. MODEL
This illustration also applies to the 4·93 h.p. Models, S30-12 and S30-13

scraper acting on the flywheels. Quick release oil level indicator of dipper type.

TRANSMISSION. Front chain $\frac{1}{2}$ in. × ·305 in., is totally enclosed and lubricated from the engine. The rear chain, $\frac{5}{8}$ in. × $\frac{3}{8}$ in., is protected by an efficient guard. Cam-faced cush drive on engine shaft. The clutch is contained in the large chain wheel, with quick adjustment, and is of the floating dry-plate type, controlled by a lever on the left-hand side of the handlebar. The B.S.A. three-speed gear-box is fitted with pivot mounting for chain adjustment, while the kick-starter mechanism is enclosed in the gear-box, and the spindle increased in diameter. An inclined gear lever is fitted on the right-hand side of the tank. The gear ratios are: solo, 5·3, 7·2, and 12·6 to 1; sidecar, 5·9, 8·0, and 13·9 to 1.

FRAME. Of new design, it possesses immense strength without excessive weight. The top member is a single high-tensile steel forging with integral head and seat lugs. Weldless steel tubing for the remainder of the frame is used. Duplex front down tubes terminate in steel forgings which are bolted to registers on the top frame member, while duplex seat tubes are set forward to accommodate the battery under the saddle. The B.S.A. spring forks with quickly adjustable shock absorbers of increased size are fitted. The head is fitted with a B.S.A. steering damper, and integral lugs for a sidecar attachment. Handlebar, touring or sports, with special mounting behind head. The saddle tank is finished in the usual B.S.A. colours (for fuel only), with a capacity of

Fig. 7. The 5·57 h.p. Model
This illustration also applies with minor differences to the 4·93 h.p. Models and 5·57 Model

2¼ gal. New pattern B.S.A. adjustable knee-grips. Tyres, 26 in. × 3·25 in., mounted on heavy gauge 19 in. × 2½ in. rims. Both brakes 7 in. diameter are quickly adjustable. Brake cams are increased in width. The front mudguard is made with flared wings, and the rear guard is hinged to allow easy removal of the wheel in conjunction with the new low-lift rear spring-up stand.

EQUIPMENT. De luxe type spring seat saddle; complete set of tools in a neat leather roll; tool-box of increased capacity and improved in appearance to conform to the lines of the machine; inflator. Footrests are standard.

FINISH. Chrominium plating to silencing system, handlebar and fittings, gear lever and quadrant, etc.

The 4·93 h.p. Model. This is a lighter model than the 4·93 h.p. de luxe, but is similar in specification, except for the following. The front brake is 5½ in. diameter; the front fork is of the new design to suit the 5½ in. brake; the saddle is the standard spring

THE VARIOUS B.S.A. MOUNTS

seat; rear chain ⅝ in. × ¼ in.; a lighter type of clutch; a priming device is not fitted; tyres, 26 in. × 3 in. All the bright parts are nickel-plated; the gear ratios are: solo, 5·2, 7·1, and 12·3 to 1; sidecar, 5·7, 7·8, and 13·5 to 1.

The 5·57 h.p. de Luxe Model. The only points of difference between this model and the 4·93 h.p. S30-9 de luxe are that the engine is 557 c.c. side valve, 85 × 98 mm. bore and stroke. The gear ratios are: solo, 5·0, 6·9, and 11·9; sidecar, 5·9, 8·0, and

FIG. 8. THE 7·70 H.P. MODEL
This illustration also applies to the 9·86 Model, G30-15

13·9 to 1; and the foot-boards are a fixed type of pressed steel construction, with pyramid rubber mats.

The 5·57 h.p. Model. This model is identical with the 4·93 h.p. S30-7, except for the 5·57 h.p. engine, 85 × 98 mm. bore and stroke; and gear ratios: solo, 5·0, 6·8, and 11·8 to 1; sidecar, 5·7, 7·8, and 13·5 to 1.

The 7·70 h.p. Model. ENGINE. 50° Vee-twin cylinder, with side valves, 7·70 h.p., 76 × 85 mm. bore and stroke. The engine actually develops 18 brake horse-power. Two rows of caged roller bearings to each connecting rod big-end. Valves protected by aluminium covers. The mainshafts are mounted on ball bearings. Special hard aluminium alloy pistons are employed.

LUBRICATION. Gravity feed from tank to mechanical pump then to sight-feed on tank, and feeding to crankcase. A hand-pump is also fitted. Oil supplied to the front chain by depressing spring by-pass valve on the timing case.

TRANSMISSION. Front chain ½ in. × ·305 in., is totally enclosed, and the rear chain ⅜ in. × ⅜ in., is protected by a guard. Cam-faced cush drive on engine shaft. The clutch is contained in the large chain wheel, with provision for quick adjustment, and is of the floating dry-plate indestructible type, controlled by a lever on the left-hand side of the handlebar. The B.S.A. three-speed gear-box is fitted, and the gear ratios are: solo, 4·2, 5·8, and 10·0 to 1; sidecar, 4·6, 6·3, and 10·9 to 1.

FRAME. All the lugs are machined from high tensile steel forgings, and special heavy gauge weldless steel tubing is used through-

FIG. 9. THE 9·86 H.P. MODEL, G30-16

out. Wheelbase, 57¾ in. The B.S.A. spring forks with quickly adjustable shock absorbers of increased size are fitted, and the head is fitted with a B.S.A. steering damper, and lugs for a sidecar attachment, integral with the frame. The handlebar is a touring or sports pattern, adjustable and mounted behind the head. The saddle tank holds 2¼ gal. of petrol and 3½ pints of oil, with gear change lever mounted on the right-hand side. New pattern B.S.A. adjustable knee-grips. Tyres, 26 in. × 3·25 in., mounted on heavy gauge 19 in. × 2¼ in. rims. Both brakes 7 in. diameter are quickly adjustable, the brake cams being increased in width. The front mudguard is made with flared wings, and the rear guard is hinged to allow easy removal of the wheel in conjunction with the new low-lift spring-up stand.

EQUIPMENT. De luxe type spring seat saddle; tool-box of improved appearance to conform to the lines of the machine; complete set of tools in a neat leather roll; inflator.

The 9·86 h.p. Model. This model is similar to the 7·70 h.p. model E30-14, but is fitted with a 9·86 h.p. engine 80 × 98 mm. bore and stroke, the engine developing 24 brake horse-power.

THE VARIOUS B.S.A. MOUNTS

The 9·86 h.p. Model. This model is suitable for exceptionally heavy sidecar duty, and has a similar specification to the 7·70 h.p. model E30-14, except that the engine is 9·86 h.p. (986 c.c.) 80 × 98 mm. bore and stroke. The engine actually develops 24 brake horse-power. The frame provides a wheelbase of 63 in., instead of 57¾ in., and is of extra heavy construction throughout with massive forged steel chainstay bridge and wide forks. The ground clearance is 5¼ in., and the saddle height is 29 in. Transmission: extra heavy gear-box suitable for a large passenger and commercial loads. The primary chain is ⅝ in. × ⅜ in. Wheels: quickly adjustable and interchangeable, with 28 in. 3·5 in. tyres. The tank is of the saddle type, with a petrol capacity of 3 gal., and oil 3½ pints. Right-hand gear change is standard. The gear ratios are solo, 4·5, 7·1, and 11·4; sidecar, 4·9, 7·9, and 12·7.

The 9 h.p. B.S.A. Three-wheeler. This B.S.A. innovation is a two-seater designed to meet the demand for more comfort and protection than is available from a motor-cycle. It is faster, lighter, simpler, and less costly in upkeep than the orthodox small car. It is a three-wheeler, employing front wheel drive, and has the following advantages over the usual rear wheel drive. It concentrates the whole of the mechanism under the bonnet, where it is readily accessible and prevents wheel spin and skidding, making the car very fast and safe, especially on corners; it also minimizes tyre wear by comparison with rear wheel drives. One reason why the B.S.A. is a three-wheeler and under 8 cwt., is in order that its tax may be only £4, although it has a 9 h.p. engine. A fourth wheel might be considered to be superfluous on a front wheel drive two-seater. One of the most important features of the design of the B.S.A. Three-wheeler is that it incorporates car type controls having a reverse in addition to three forward speeds, and a pedal accelerator. The ignition timing and the slow running adjustment of the throttle are on the steering column. The pedal brake acts on all wheels, the hand brake acting on the rear wheel only. The steering itself is extraordinarily good.

ENGINE. 9 h.p. air-cooled 90° Vee-twin 85 × 90 mm. 1021 c.c. Solex carburettor with exhaust hot spot and aluminium alloy pistons. Overhead valves of special steel, operated by enclosed and efficiently lubricated rockers and push-rods; roller bearings are fitted to the crankshaft and connecting rod big-ends, and a steel flywheel is employed.

LUBRICATION. Five pints of oil are contained in a sump that is integral with the crankcase, and in which is a submerged gear type pump driven by worm gear from the crankshaft. A dip stick is fitted for measuring the oil level in the sump, and the oil pressure is maintained by the pump and automatically controlled by a by-pass valve. Oil is delivered direct to the cylinder walls and the timing gear, the supply being controlled by a valve on the timing cover. This valve is correctly set during test and normally requires no further adjustment.

TRANSMISSION. The clutch is of the floating plate type with cork insets. Over-filling is prevented by a level plug. The gearbox contains three forward speeds and reverse, the ratios of

FIG. 10. THE 9 H.P. THREE-WHEELER,
WITH FRONT-WHEEL DRIVE

which are approximately $5\frac{1}{4}$, 8, 15, and 18 respectively. Central control. Worm gear drive to the front axle with spur type differential. From the differential the drive is transmitted to the front wheel through strong flexible couplings and universal joints.

FRAME AND SUSPENSION. The engine and transmission are supported on a channel section steel frame, but the side members of this converge at the back on to a very strong steel tube, terminating in a bracket supporting a cantilever on which the rear wheel is mounted. The inner end of this cantilever carries a quarter eliptic spring projecting inside the tubes on to which the front end of the spring abuts through a felt-lined steel slipper. The spring is attached to the slipper by a silent-bloc bearing which requires no lubrication. The felt lining of the slipper is saturated with grease before assembly, and therefore requires only occasional lubrication, provision for which is made by means of a grease gun nipple on the side of the tube. The front wheels are independently sprung, each being supported on 4 quarter eliptic springs which take the place of the axle casting in an ordinary car. Dampers are fitted to all wheels. The wheels are made of

THE VARIOUS B.S.A. MOUNTS

heavy gauge 19 in. × 3 in. rims with double butted spokes, and they are fitted with large Dunlop tyres 27 in. × 4 in. They are quickly detachable and interchangeable. Over-all length 10 ft. 6 in. with B.S.A. body. Over-all width 4 ft. 10 in. Wheelbase 7 ft. 4 in.

BRAKES. The brakes are of the internal expanding type and large in diameter. That on the differential controls both front wheels, there being another brake acting on the rear wheel. The pedal controls both brakes simultaneously, thus retarding the car on all wheels, the hand brake operating on the rear wheel only. It is intended primarily as a parking brake, but can be used in addition to the pedal at any time. The brake lever is on the driver's right.

B.S.A. SIDECARS

When ordering B.S.A. sidecars separately from a motor-cycle, it is essential that the type and year of machine should be quoted, as in some cases different front stays, front support tubes, and saddle pillar tubes are required to suit each type. Full details and part numbers of the connections required will be found in the special chart issued to B.S.A. dealers. Fork links of special length marked "Sidecar" are provided on 4·93 h.p., 5·57 h.p., and 7·70 h.p. models when these are ordered for sidecar work. When these machines are used for solo work, links of standard length must be used.

Nos. 6 and 6a Sidecars. No. 6 sidecar is suitable for models S30-9, H30-10, S30-12, S30-13, E30-14, G30-15, and G30-16, whereas No. 6a is suitable for G30-16 model only.

The chassis is of triangular construction and is attached to the motor-cycle frame at four points, the front of the body being supported by a helical spring. At the rear the body is clamped to a transverse semi-elliptic spring, the ends of which are attached to the twin axle tubes on the chassis, the left-hand end being shackled. Shackles are fitted with grease gun nipples, and a stand is fitted to the sidecar wheel. The body is coach-finished in dark green, with dark green buttonless upholstery and arm rests. A spring-seat cushion is fitted, and the back is also sprung. A map pocket is provided, and under the seat is a tool locker. In the back of the body is a roomy luggage compartment constructed to accommodate a child's seat, seat and squab being extra. A windscreen and waterproof apron are fitted to this sidecar as standard. A 5½-in. diameter brake to the sidecar wheel can be fitted as an extra.

The No. 6a sidecar is the same as No. 6, but is fitted to a spring wheel chassis, increasing the comfort of both passenger and driver. A 7-in. diameter brake to the sidecar wheel can be fitted as an extra.

Nos. 7 and 7c Sidecars. These are suitable for Model No. L30-11 and larger models.

FIG. 11. B.S.A. NO. 6. SIDECAR

FIG. 12. B.S.A. NO. 7 SIDECAR

The No. 7 chassis is similar to the No. 6, but it has been slightly modified to give a narrower wheel track, a great advantage on a

THE VARIOUS B.S.A. MOUNTS

sporting chassis. Grease gun nipples are fitted to the end of the springshackle bolts. The body is coach-finished in a rich shade of dark green. The upholstery is buttonless, and arm rests are fitted. There is a lock-up luggage compartment behind the fixed seat back, and a luggage platform on top of the locker. A waterproof apron is fitted.

The chassis of No. 7c sidecar is identical with No. 7, but the

FIG. 13. B.S.A. SIDECAR NO. 14

body has no door, and the locker space is behind the removable seat back.

Nos. 9 and 9c Sidecars. These are suitable for models L30-6 and S30-18 only.

The bodies are the same as for numbers 7 and 7c, respectively, but the chassis is of lighter and more simple construction.

Nos. 14 and 15 Sidecars. No. 15 sidecar is suitable for Model No. L30-11, and larger models, whereas No. 14 is suitable for Model S30-18 only.

These are De Luxe Sports model sidecars built with polished aluminium panels. The body is octagonal in section, tapering to a point at the rear to reduce wind resistance to a minimum. The hinged dash is provided with a glove box, and allows easy entrance and exit. The windscreen is fitted as standard. Luggage space is provided behind the hinged seat-back, and a waterproof apron is supplied. The chassis of No. 15 sidecar is identical with **No. 7**, while No. 14 sidecar is mounted on a No. 9 chassis. These sidecars can be supplied finished in a special smart colour scheme, with top centre panel dark green and the panel on either side of it in cream, at an extra charge.

PERFORMANCE FIGURES OF B.S.A. MOTOR-CYCLES

Model	Max. speed on level M.P.H.	Min. M.P.G. of oil which should be obtained.	M.P.G. of petrol at 25-30 M.P.H.
1·74 h.p.	38–43	2,200	120–140
2·49 h.p. S.V.	43–47	2,000–3,000	100–120
2·49 h.p. O.H.V.	58–64	2,000–3,000	100–130
3·49 h.p. S.V.	50–55	2,000–3,000	95–115
3·49 h.p. S.V. Commercial (L30-6)	40–45	1,500–2,000	75–80
3·49 h.p. O.H.V. Solo (high-compression piston)	70–75	2,000–3,000	105–125
3·49 h.p. O.H.V. (high-compression piston), with No. 15 Sidecar	55–60	1,500–2,000	80–85
4·93 h.p. S.V. Solo	58–62	2,000–3,000	85–100
4·93 h.p. S.V., with No. 7 Sidecar	46–50	1,500–2,000	65–75
4·93 h.p. O.H.V. Solo	70–75	2,000–3,000	85–100
4·93 h.p. O.H.V., with No. 15 Sidecar	60–65	1,500–2,000	65–80
4·93 h.p. O.H.V. Solo (high-compression piston)	78–82	2,000–3,000	85–100
4·93 h.p. O.H.V. (high-compression piston), with No. 15 Sidecar	65–70	1,500–2,000	65–80
5·57 h.p. S.V., with No. 6 Sidecar	45–50	1,500–2,000	60–65
7·70 h.p. Solo	68–73	2,000	70–80
7·70 h.p. S.V., with No. 6 Sidecar	52–57	1,500	55–65
9·86 h.p. S.V., with No. 6 Sidecar	62–68	1,500	55–60

HORSE-POWER AND COMPRESSION RATIO

Model.	Compression Ratio.	Maximum Brake h.p.	At Revs.
1·74 h.p.	4·5	4·6	4,200
2·49 h.p. S.V.	4·8	6·0	4,400
2·49 h.p. O.H.V.	5·5	10·8	5,400
3·49 h.p. S.V.	4·5	8·0	4,400
3·49 h.p. O.H.V.	5·4 or 7	18·0	5,200
4·93 h.p. S.V.	4·4	12·0	4,200
4·93 h.p. O.H.V.	5·8 or 6·8	27·0	5,000
5·57 h.p. S.V.	4·2	12·0	4,000
7·70 h.p. S.V.	4·5	18·0	3,800
9·86 h.p. S.V.	4·4	24·0	3,600

The maximum engine revolutions are greatly in excess of the revolutions given above.

GEAR RATIOS OF B.S.A. MOTOR-CYCLES

Model.	Solo Machines (Gt. Britain). Teeth on Engine Sprocket.	High.	Middle.	Low.	Solo Machines (Overseas). Teeth on Engine Sprocket.	High.	Middle	Low.	Sidecar Machines. Teeth on Engine Sprocket.	High.	Middle.	Low.
1·74 h.p. S.V.	16	6·8	10·3	14	16	6·8	10·3	14	—	—	—	—
2·49 h.p. S.V.	17	6·2	9·3	13·6	16	6·6	9·8	14·5	—	—	—	—
2·49 h.p. O.H.V.	17	6·2	9·3	13·6	16	6·6	9·8	14·5	—	—	—	—
3·49 h.p. S.V.	19	5·6	8·2	12·1	18	5·9	8·7	12·8	—	—	—	—
3·49 h.p. S.V.	19	5·6	8·2	12·1	18	5·9	8·7	12·8	16	6·6	9·8	14·5
4·93 h.p. O.H.V.*	21	5·7	7·8	13·5	21	5·7	7·8	13·5	20	6·0	8·2	14·3
4·93 h.p. S.V. Light	24	5·0	6·8	11·8	23	5·2	7·1	12·3	21	5·7	7·8	13·5
4·93 h.p. S.V.†	23	5·2	7·1	12·3	23	5·2	7·1	12·3	21	5·7	7·8	13·5
4·93 h.p. S.V. de Luxe	20	5·3	7·2	12·6	20	5·3	7·2	12·6	18	5·9	8·0	1·39
4·93 h.p. O.H.V. Light }												
4·93 h.p. O.H.V.* }	22	4·8	6·6	11·4	21	5·0	6·9	11·9	19	5·6	7·6	13·2
4·93 h.p. O.H.V. de Luxe	24	5·0	6·8	11·8	24	5·0	6·8	11·8	21	5·7	7·8	13·5
5·57 h.p. S.V.†	21	5·0	6·9	11·9	21	5·0	6·9	11·9	18	5·9	8·0	13·9
5·57 h.p. S.V. de Luxe†												
7·70 h.p. S.V. }												
9·86 h.p. S.V. }	25	4·2	5·8	10·0	24	4·4	6·0	10·4	23	4·6	6·3	10·9
9·86 h.p. S.V. W.T.	20	4·5	7·1	11·4	20	4·5	7·1	11·4	18	4·9	7·9	12·7

* A special close or wide ratio gear-box can be fitted to these models if desired.
† A special wide ratio gear-box for sidecar work can be fitted to these models, if specified.

CHAPTER II

REGISTRATION, DRIVING LICENCE AND EQUIPMENT

IN this chapter, the writer pre-supposes that the reader, having selected the mount to suit his inclinations, now turns to the question of the necessary legal formalities and requirements to be satisfied before the machine may be taken on the road.

The Driving Licence. This licence must be in the possession of all drivers of motor vehicles when driving, and it must be produced when the request is made by a police officer. The mere possession of the licence, be it noted, does not discharge liability, for it must be carried whilst driving the vehicle. *It may not be lent* to any person for the purpose of driving the owner's machine. As the law stands at present, any person over the age of 14 can obtain a driving licence, although legislation is shortly to be introduced which will raise the age limit from 14 to 16 years. The licence, therefore, is no indication of ability, but merely an index or receipt for tax paid. It is procurable from the local Borough or County Council office, and it costs 5s. per year, the year counting from the date on which the licence is issued until the corresponding date of the subsequent year. There is no need to apply personally for it—application may be made by post—but personal application saves time, especially if an entry on the official application form is likely to be queried. If the reader is over 17 years of age, it is best to make application for a licence to drive a motor-car, which entitles the holder to drive any motor-car or motor-cycle, whereas a driving licence applying to motor-cycles alone restricts the holder to that type of vehicle. If the reader at the time of application is over 14 but under 17, he may only apply for a motor-cycle driver's licence.

Registration and Tax. All motor-cycles must be registered at the local Borough or County Council office, and if the machine is to be used on the public roads a tax, according to its weight, must be paid on it; a part of the application form is given on page 21, showing the amount.

It will be seen that the licence may be taken out annually, quarterly, or part yearly, as detailed later on. For the purpose of the law, the term *weight unladen* is taken to mean the machine in its running condition, and does not include the tool kit, petrol,

REGISTRATION, DRIVING LICENCE, ETC.   21

accumulators, or water, but it does include headlamp and generator (whether acetylene or electric) horn, and the rear lamp and their connections. The licence (a circular label on which is entered details of machine, date, and amount of tax paid) must be exhibited in a conspicuous position on the near-side (left-hand side when seated on the saddle), and be carried in a weather-proof holder with transparent front so as clearly to be visible by daylight to a person standing at the near-side of the vehicle. Only *two* positions are sanctioned by the authorities; on the near side of the handlebar or on the near-side of the combination.

I apply for a licence expiring on 19.. for a:	Annual Licences expiring on 31st December.	Quarterly licences expiring on 24th March, 30th June, 30th Sept. or 31st December.
MOTOR-CYCLE (or motor scooter or cycle with auto-wheel or other motor attachment:		
Note: Motor-cycles exceeding 8 cwt. in weight unladen are chargeable to duty as cars.	Duty. £ s. d.	Duty. £ s. d.
(a) Bicycle:—		
Weight unladen, not exceeding 224 lb.	1 10 -	8 3
Weight unladen, not exceeding 224 lb. with right to draw trailer or sidecar	2 10 -	13 9
Weight unladen exceeding 224 lb., but not exceeding 8 cwt.	3 - -	16 6
Weight unladen exceeding 224 lb. with right to draw trailer or sidecar	4 - -	1 2 -
(b) Tricycle (not exceeding 8 cwt. in weight unladen	4 - -	1 2 -

A registration book is issued with the licence, and in it is entered full particulars of the machine, as well as conditions of renewal of the licence.

Surrender Value. Every licence now has a surrender value; for details apply to the issuing council.

Renewal Before Expiry of Old Licence. A licence may be renewed as early as fourteen days before the expiration of the old licence, and it is advised that advantage be taken of this arrangement.

Licences are renewable by post. Applications should be addressed to offices of the County Council, and must be accompanied by form R.F. 1A (or the appropriate form in the case of re-declarations) and the necessary remittance for duty. A licence cannot be renewed on a letter of request only.

Exceptions to Renewal at a Post Office. Licences are renewable at the principal money order post offices, except in the following cases: First licences for vehicles not already registered;

licences subject to rebate on pre-1913 engines; renewal of licences which have expired more than fourteen days previously; annual licences where the last licences were quarterly, and vice versa; licences for vehicles which have changed ownership since the last licences were issued; in cases where the registered owners of the vehicle have changed their addresses, or where any particulars of the vehicles have been changed since the last licences were issued; applications for the renewal of licences where page 7 of the relative registration book is filled up; trade licences.

Replacing a Lost Book. If by any chance the registration book has been mislaid or lost, then the licensing authority, upon payment of a fee of 5s., will issue a fresh registration book.

If the licence itself has been lost or has become illegible through rain or sun, then it must be immediately returned to be replaced. To ride a motor-cycle with an illegible licence is an offence for which the rider can be convicted and fined. A duplicate can be obtained from the registration authority, but the fee of 5s. will again be demanded unless it is possible to satisfy the authority that the illegibility or fading is not due to any neglect or carelessness.

Regarding the Registration Book. Upon the first issue of the registration book sign your name in the top space provided on page 3. Keep the book in a safe place, not on the vehicle. If you lose the book, you may have trouble and delay in renewing the licence or in disposing of the vehicle; and you should report the loss at once to your registration authority.

If the particulars on page 6 of the book are not correct, inform the registration authority at once.

If you make any change in your vehicle which affects the particulars on page 6 you must at once inform your registration authority and send the book to them. It is an offence not to notify any change of the registration particulars. You must at the same time send the licence when the alteration affects any of the particulars thereon. If the alteration made increases the amount of licence duty payable, you should send a cheque for the amount of the additional duty.

Renewal of Licence. When your licence expires, if the vehicle has not changed hands since the licence was issued, get a renewal form (R.F. 1A) from your registration authority or from a money order post office, and fill it in. You should then send it to the registration authority or take it to a principal post office in the area of your registration authority, together with the proper duty, when you will get the registration book back, with a new licence.

REGISTRATION, DRIVING LICENCE, ETC. 23

Where renewal is effected at a post office, the old licence must be surrendered at the time of application; in other cases it must be destroyed on expiry. If the last licence was not taken out by you, the vehicle must be fully declared on the appropriate declaration form before a new licence can be obtained.

If the licence is not renewed owing to the non-use of the vehicle, you must retain this registration book and produce it to the registration authority when you apply at a subsequent date for another licence for the same vehicle. When a vehicle is broken up, destroyed, or sent permanently out of Great Britain, the registration book must be surrendered to your registration authority.

Change of Address. If you change your permanent address, at once put your name and new address in Block Capitals in the first vacant " CHANGE " space on page 3 (or 4, if 3 is filled), sign your name below it and post the book to the registration authority whose address is given on page 2.

Transfer of Vehicle. On transferring the vehicle to another person, you must hand over this book to the person acquiring the vehicle. At the same time you must notify in writing (either by letter or on the form mentioned below) the registration authority, whose address is given on page 2, that the vehicle has been handed over, and the notification must contain the following information: The index mark and number of the vehicle; the make and class of vehicle; and the name and address of the person to whom the vehicle was handed over.

A form (R.F. 70) may be obtained for this purpose from any money order post office.

A person acquiring a vehicle and intending to use it upon the public roads (otherwise than under a Trade Licence) must, as soon as he acquires the vehicle, fill up the first vacant " CHANGE" space on page 3 (or 4, if 3 is filled), giving his full name, address, and usual signature, and post this book to the registration authority whose address is given on page 2 of the book. The registration will then be transferred to his name.

Dealers Who Buy to Sell Again. If the person acquiring this vehicle does not intend to use it upon the public roads (otherwise than under a Trade Licence) but to dispose of it to a third party, he need not send in the book or fill in a " CHANGE " space. He must, however, as soon as he acquires the vehicle, notify in writing the registration authority, whose address is given on page 2 of the book, that he holds the vehicle but does not intend to use it on the public roads. He must also comply with instruction above, on transferring the vehicle to another person. (The procedure outlined in this paragraph is designed to meet the case of dealers and other persons who do not intend to use the vehicle but to dispose of it.)

Part-year Licences. Motor-cycle licences can now be taken out for any number of months, varying from four to eleven, and expiring on 31st December, at one-twelfth the annual rate of duty for each month of the currency of the licence, plus a surcharge of 5 per cent. This is in itself a concession, as hitherto the only

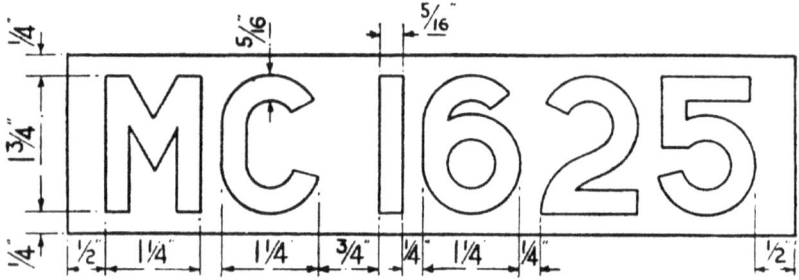

FIG. 14. FRONT NUMBER PLATE DIMENSIONS

available short period motor-cycle licences, for one, two, or three quarters, have involved a surcharge of 10 per cent.

An example of the operation of the new part-year licensing scheme is found in the case of a motor-cyclist desirous of taking out a licence for a motor-cycle from 1st June to the end of the year. For a machine weighing over 224 lb. the tax on which would be £3 per annum, the licence duty payable for the seven months is £1 16s. 9d. made up as follows—

	£	s.	d.
Seven-twelfths of £3	1	15	0
Add 5 per cent		1	9
	£1	16	9

Under the old system, the motor-cyclist would have had to take out a licence from 25th March to December 31st, costing £2 9s. 6d., or defer putting the machine on the road until 1st July and licence it for two quarters at a cost of £1 13s. 0d.

Although this new licensing scheme is limited in its scope in that the shortest period allowed is four months, motor-cyclists desirous of laying up their machines during the tail end of the season may do so by surrendering their licences and obtaining a rebate on the unexpired portion. By this means a refund can

REGISTRATION, DRIVING LICENCE, ETC.

be obtained for each complete month of the period of the currency of the licence which is unexpired, the refund being calculated *pro rata* plus a fee of 5s.

Number Plates. This simple item of the equipment is hedged round with restrictions. One must be provided at the front and rear of the machine, and upon them must be painted the registered numbers which have been assigned to the machine and which are entered on the registration label and also in the registration book. The numbers must conform to the following proportions : Each

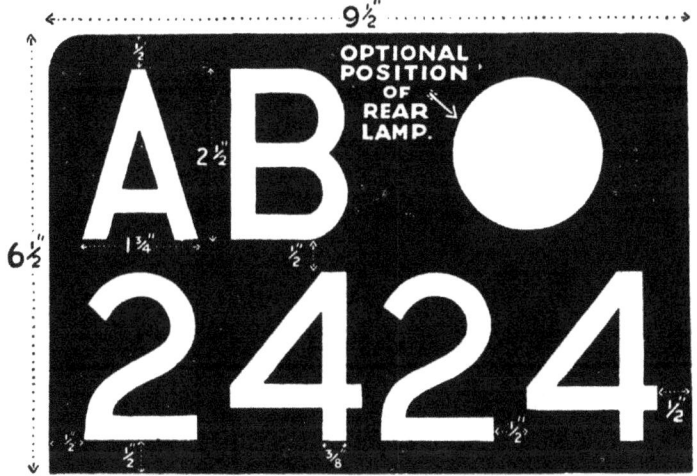

FIG. 15. REAR NUMBER PLATE DIMENSIONS

figure or letter must be $2\frac{1}{2}$ in. by $1\frac{3}{4}$ in. wide, and $\frac{3}{8}$ in. thick at all parts (see Fig. 15). Between the top and bottom of the letters and the edge of the plate there must be a margin of at least $\frac{1}{2}$ in., with a margin of $\frac{1}{2}$ in. at each side. The letters must be in white on a black ground, and they must not be permitted to become obscured by mud or dust ; nor must the view of them be obstructed by any person or article on the machine.

Lamps. During the period between one hour after sunset and one hour before sunrise (see time table on page 117) it is compulsory to show a white light at the front of the machine, and, in addition, both solo and sidecar machines must show a red light at the rear. Red reflectors are not sufficient. Lamps which remain alight only while the engine is running are illegal unless a stand-by battery is fitted to light the lamps when the engine has stopped. One number plate must be illuminated—it does not matter whether front or rear. If the machine is a combination this also must have a lamp showing white forward, and it must be fixed in such a way that from the front and in conjunction with the headlamp it fairly indicates the extreme width of the vehicle, i.e. on sidecar mudguard.

Audible Warning of Approach. A horn, either of the mechanical or the bulb type, must be fitted so that adequate and audible warning of approach may be given to pedestrians, as well as to the drivers of other vehicles. Preference is given to an electric horn yielding a deep, sonorous note.

It may be taken that legal matters regarding the machine itself, such as silencing, brakes, etc., have been attended to by the makers, and there is little need to reiterate such regulations here.

JOINING A CLUB

There can be no question that many advantages may be derived from joining either the A.C.U. (Auto-Cycle Union), the A.A. (Automobile Association), or the R.A.C. (Royal Automobile Club). Free legal advice and defence, " get-you-home " scheme, services of road guides and local consuls, touring and technical assistance, and insurance facilities are available for a nominal annual subscription. The addresses of the above clubs are given hereunder. Membership of the A.C.U. can only be obtained through membership of a club affiliated to the A.C.U.

Auto-Cycle Union,
83 Pall Mall,
London, S.W.1.

Royal Automobile Club,
89-91 Pall Mall,
London, S.W.1.

Automobile Association,
Fanum House,
New Coventry Street,
London, W.1.

INSURANCE

It is not compulsory for one to insure against loss by fire, personal injury by accident, injury to others (third party risks), injury to machine, loss of machine by theft, but it is beyond all cavil that it is wise to do so.

The Comprehensive Policy. Three classes of insurance policies are issued by the insurance companies for the benefit of motor-cyclists. The first covers up to an unlimited amount, the owner's legal liability to the public for injury to person and damage to property, and includes all the legal costs incurred with the company's consent. Additionally, it covers the cost of legal representation at police courts or inquests in connection with an accident covered by the policy, loss or damage caused by fire, lightning, explosion, self-ignition, or by burglary, house-breaking, or theft. It also covers loss or damage arising from an accidental explosion, or from wilful or malicious acts, or whilst in transit.

Part Cover. Many motor-cyclists, however, prefer to make themselves responsible for the damage caused by a collision, and to meet this, the insurance companies provide a policy appropriately phrased omitting reference to damage arising from accidental collision, etc. Yet other motor-cyclists also prefer to run the fire and theft risks as well, and so a policy is issued which also has no reference to fire and theft. The following table gives details of the three policies and their costs—

	Not exceeding 200 c.c.	Not exceeding 350 c.c.	Not exceeding 750 c.c.	Exceeding 750 c.c.
	£ s. d.	£ s. d.	£ s. d.	£ s. d.
Comprehensive benefits 1, 2, 3, and 4 . .	3 - -	3 15 -	6 - -	7 10 -
	If value exceeds £50 then additional premium is payable at the rate of 20s. per cent on value in excess of £50.			
Public, liability, fire and theft, benefits 1, 2, and 3 . . .	1 10 -	1 15 -	2 - -	2 5 -
	If value exceeds £50 then additional premium is payable at the rate of 15s. per cent on value in excess of £50.			
Public, liability, benefits 1 and 2 . . .	15 -	1 - -	1 5 -	1 10 -
	Irrespective of value.			

What the Policy Does not Cover. Under these policies the premiums quoted apply only when the motor-cycle is used for pleasure, and is ridden only by the owner. If it is intended that the machine should be ridden by any other person or persons, as well as the owner, add $33\frac{1}{3}$ per cent for one driver who must be named or 50 per cent for any driver. Solo machines may not carry a pillion passenger unless that clause has been inserted at the request of the insured. Machines used for business purposes may be covered at a special rate according to circumstances. If the motor-cycle is used for racing, pacemaking, trials, or is let out on hire, the policy ceases to operate, nor does it enable a claim to be made for replacements rendered necessary by wear and tear, break-downs, damage to tyres caused by skids, application of brakes, punctures, or bursts.

Insurance Conditions. These are usually simple. The first condition is that the company shall be advised of all accidents immediately. Secondly, that the insured or his agents shall not make any admission of liability to, or negotiate with any third parties, and that he and his agents shall render all reasonable assistance to the company to negotiate, resist, or settle any such claims, the company reserving the right to settle or otherwise deal with such claims at their sole discretion.

The insured shall submit estimates for the repairs of the machine to the company for approval. Generally speaking, reasonable repairs can be authorized by the owner provided no new parts are necessary.

CHAPTER III

DRIVING

It is worth while giving a few minutes' thought and experiment to the various controls, before actually driving the machine.

Place the machine on the stand by placing the foot against it as it rests on the ground and pulling the machine back by means of the back fork stays or lifting handle. Do *not* pull it back by means of the saddle, for you may, in the course of time, break a saddle spring by such practice. Now remove the filler cap and fill the petrol tank and also the oil tank or sump (except in the case of the two-stroke, which employs petroil lubrication). Remove the filler cap from the right-hand end of the gear-box, and insert cylinder oil of the grade recommended for the model, until it comes level with the lip of the filler spout and no more can be poured in. Then replace the cap and tighten up with a spanner.

Lubricating the Engine. This is one of the most important points to be remembered in managing a motor-cycle. Whilst it is true that the engine will not run until it has a supply of petrol, it is equally true that it will not run *very long* unless it is kept well supplied with lubricating oil. The friction of the different parts would cause some of the softer metals employed in the bearings to get hot and expand beyond the working point, and the engine would stop suddenly with the bearings or the connecting rod damaged. This is what is technically known as "seizing up." On those models fitted with sight feed and mechanical pump (the 493 c.c. S.V. light, the 493 O.H.V. light, and the 770 c.c. and 986 c.c. twin cylinder models) the first thing to do is to open the supply valve of the lubricating system a few turns, and push down the pump plunger smartly until it remains down. The barrel is then charged and oil flows through the sight feed. When the plunger rises to the top the pump is empty. Repeat this operation three or four times. The engine will then be sufficiently charged for starting, and the drip may be set at the desired flow by adjustment of the valve. Make certain that the oil tap is " on " if a tap is fitted. Some models are not provided with a tap.

Before a new machine is run for the first time it is necessary to give the engine a supply of oil. The most convenient way to do this is to remove the sparking plug and turn the engine until the piston is at the bottom of its stroke. Then pour a small quantity of oil (not more than about two teaspoonfuls) into the cylinder through the sparking plug hole. Allow the machine to stand for a few minutes before starting up. This will provide the necessary lubrication while the pump is delivering oil from the sump. It is only necessary to oil in this manner when starting a new engine for the first time.

On the sump lubricated models the oil supply is controlled by a valve on the delivery side of the pump, the operation of which is, fully described in Chapter V. This should be studied before the engine is started.

Petrol Supply to the Engine. The next thing to do is to turn on the petrol by turning the lever to the position marked ON. When a priming tap is fitted (it is not fitted to all models) the tap is off when it is pointing vertically downwards. If moved upwards towards the front, it allows the petrol to flow along the priming tube; while if moved upwards towards the back, it turns the petrol on to the carburettor as explained above.

The Various Controls and Their Purpose. The three main controls to the engine are: (1) the gas supply, (2) the air supply, (3) the spark control for advancing and retarding the spark. There are also one or two minor controls, such as the exhaust lifter, which is used chiefly for starting. These are described in detail later. Another most important control is the clutch. This is simply a device for disconnecting the drive from the engine to the gear-box at will, so that the engine can run without causing any movement of the machine. The gears are controlled by the gear lever, which will be found on the right-hand side of the machine. Anyone who has ridden a three-speed gear bicycle will know why gears are necessary. The low gear is to make matters easier for the engine when the machine is travelling up a steep hill. The second gear is for easing matters on a hill which does not tax the engine to its utmost. The top gear is for normal travelling on the level or up slight inclines and also for travelling down hill. We shall have more to say about the intelligent use of the gears a little later.

Operating the Controls for Starting the Engine. Open the throttle lever, which is the lower of the two control levers on the right handlebar, a distance equal to about one-third of its full movement. Leave the air lever shut; remember that some controls open outwards, and some inwards. The air lever is the upper and shorter of the two levers. The lever above the left handlebar is the spark advance lever, which on most of the models advances towards the tank. Set this at about two-thirds advance, that is two-thirds of its total travel from its extreme left-hand position. Now pull up the exhaust release lever on the left-hand side of the bars as far as it will go. See that the gear lever on the right-hand side of the machine is in the neutral position. If the lever should happen to be in another position, raise the exhaust-valve lifter (fitted to the left handlebar), revolve the engine by means of the kick-starter, and at the same time push the gear lever into the neutral position. Never attempt to move the gear lever while the engine is stationary.

Starting the Engine. Everything is now ready for starting the engine, and all that it is necessary to do is to push down the kick-starter pedal smartly with the foot (of course using the exhaust valve lever for a portion of the kick-starter stroke), when the engine should fire at once. Provided the instructions given above as to the setting of the various levers have been carefully followed, the engine should start at the first or second depression of the kick starter.

Priming the Engine. If the engine feels very stiff when the kick starter is depressed, it may be advisable to prime the cylinder by removing the plug from the cylinder, and allowing a few drops of petrol to run into it via the priming pipe by turning the petrol tap forwards as explained above. This will free the piston and make it more easy to operate the kick starter. Be careful not to put too much petrol into the cylinder when priming, and never prime at all unless it is really necessary.

Procedure after Engine has Started. As soon as the engine starts, open the air lever until the engine is firing regularly. It should be noted that the positions given above for the air, throttle, and spark levers are only approximate. A rider can only ascertain by experience the lever positions which enable him to start his own machine most easily. The " sound " and " feel " of a machine which will tell the rider that the engine is running well cannot be imparted by printed instructions.

The Action of the Controls. Let the engine run for a minute or two on the stand, but do not race it. Meanwhile note the results obtained by opening and shutting the throttle and air levers, advancing and retarding the spark, and operating the exhaust valve lifter, so as to become familiar with their operation.

Operating the Clutch and Gears. With the machine still on the stand and the engine still running, sit on the saddle and practise operating the clutch and gears. Raise the clutch lever on the outside of the left handlebar, and push the gear lever on the right from the neutral into the low gear position, then allow the clutch to engage by gently releasing the lever held with the left hand. The back wheel will gradually speed up, and by the time the lever has been fully lowered, the wheel will be revolving steadily. To change the gear the clutch should be disengaged and the gear lever smartly moved into the second gear position. Every time the gear is moved the clutch must be disengaged. Ten minutes spent in becoming familiar with the method of gear changing, declutching, advancing and retarding the spark, will be well worth while, otherwise on the road, especially if there is much traffic about, the novice will find it rather difficult to think of all these small items. After a little practice their use will become second nature, but it is highly desirable to make their first acquaintance in the calm security of the cycle shed or garage. If the reader has ridden an ordinary push bicycle he will find no difficulty in balancing the motor cycle, and, if anything, this will be found to be decidedly easier.

THE FIRST SPIN

Now, standing on the left-hand side of the machine, push it gently off the stand, and swing the latter up into position. (On some models a spring-up stand is fitted.) Now mount the machine, the engine being still running, raise the clutch lever (on outside of left handlebar) to its fullest extent, and push the gear lever into *low gear position*. Then engage the clutch by gently and slowly releasing the clutch lever with the left hand at the same time gradually opening the throttle, and the machine will start away smoothly and gather speed. Be careful always to disengage the clutch fully before moving the gear lever from the neutral position. Of course, when the rider is used to the machine, or if the machine has a sidecar, it is not necessary to put it on the stand to start it. The kick-starter can easily be operated by the rider when seated on the saddle.

Changing Gear. As soon as the machine is travelling at a speed of about 10 miles an hour change to second gear, next accelerate to about 20 miles per hour, and then change to top gear. Always declutch when changing gear, and having made the change let the clutch in again slowly. When reducing speed, whether because the machine is climbing a steep hill or for any other cause, never let the engine labour on top gear. As soon as the engine seems inclined to labour change down into second gear. This is done merely by lifting the clutch and pushing the gear lever smartly into the desired position. A similar operation enables the rider to change from second to low gear, if the speed similarly becomes too low for the second gear. Do **not** be **afraid**

to change to a lower gear if it is thought desirable. The gear-box is on the machine for use, and far more harm is done by letting the engine labour and thump unnecessarily on a high gear than by letting it " rev " a little on a lower gear. If very slow running is desired, as for instance when negotiating dense traffic, change into bottom gear and partly disengage the clutch. The clutch is fitted with special friction linings, and cannot be damaged by a reasonable amount of slipping when slow running is required. The point to bear in mind about gear changing is that when *changing up* the engine speed should be reduced, and when *changing down* the engine speed should be increased. This makes silent gear changing easy. The point to aim at is to get the two gear parts which have to engage to revolve at the same speed.

The Exhaust-Valve Lifter. Do not control the speed of the engine by operating the exhaust-valve lifter. The speed should always be controlled by the throttle lever, for reasons explained presently, and the exhaust lifter should only be used for starting purposes.

Coasting. When descending hills the clutch may be disengaged and the engine stopped altogether, so that the machine coasts down like a bicycle. After coasting down a hill do not attempt to start the engine by means of the clutch if the low gear is engaged or serious damage may result and you may be thrown over the handlebars. Release the clutch and engage high gear, open the throttle slightly, and let the clutch in gradually until the engine starts.

Acceleration. It is always wise when driving to avoid violent acceleration, because wheel-spin as well as skids are likely to occur, with decidedly bad effects on the tyres. Always endeavour to take up slowly and evenly, and to accelerate gradually. Whenever possible, regulate the speed by opening or closing the throttle gradually, not suddenly, and use so much air that the engine can be felt to be running under its best conditions. Do not run the engine with the air lever nearly closed for any length of time, otherwise the engine will be liable to overheat.

Lubrication Details. Watch the drip feed or the tell-tale occasionally to see if the lubrication system is working properly. A suitable setting of the drip feed system is about six notches or half a turn of the adjusting valve. Over lubrication will at once be apparent by the undue amount of smoke from the exhaust. If so, reduce the rate of drip, but always bear in mind that it is better to over lubricate than to give insufficient oil. Particularly is this so with regard to a new engine. If sufficient oil is not obtained through the mechanical pump, this should be supplemented occasionally by the hand pump.

For high speed work, an extra two notches or so may be given. At the commencement of a ride, give a charge of oil from the hand pump (when fitted) to ensure that there is a sufficiency of oil in the crankcase.

The auxiliary pump which is attached to some of the B.S.A. models is for the purpose of assisting the lubrication, and should only be used when the engine is put under particular stress, such as when climbing a fairly steep hill, or being driven at high speeds. The pump cannot, of course, be operated until the plunger is released by moving back the catch fitted to the gland nut, and the use of the auxiliary pump will in no way interfere with the working of the mechanical pump.

The Running-in Period. The life of the machine will be greatly increased if a speed of not more than 35 miles an hour in top gear is kept to for the first 500 miles, and 25 m.p.h. and 15 m.p.h. on middle and low gears, and a speed not exceeding 40 miles an hour for the next 500 miles. The running-in of a new motor-cycle may be laborious, but it will pay in the long run. Both the crankcase and the oil sump should be drawn every 1,000 miles.

The Advance and Retard. Drive with the spark in the position in which the machine accelerates best. A retarded spark causes overheating and excessive petrol consumption.

How to Stop. Having told the reader how to start and ride the machine, it is imperative that he should know how to stop it. The sequence for stopping is as follows : (1) Close throttle ; (2) raise clutch lever ; (3) apply foot-brake and/or hand-brake gradually as found necessary.

Use of the Brakes. What has been said about violent acceleration applies with equal force to the other extreme—violent braking, or deceleration. One of the most frequent causes of skidding is sudden application of the brakes, due to the locking of the wheel. It is this sudden locking which causes a skid, but whether a skid takes place or not, the effect on the tyres is bad.

Adjusting the Brakes. Occasionally it is necessary to adjust the brakes, to compensate for wear. The adjustment should be such that the brake is not rubbing the drum when in the " off " position, or power will be lost in overcoming this extra friction.

DRIVING

This can be done by placing the machine on the stand, with the gear lever in neutral, spinning the back wheel and adjusting the brakes until wear is taken up. Nor should the adjustment necessitate a comparatively large movement of the pedal before the brake comes into operation. The rods operating the front brake need attention every now and then, for they are liable to become slack. Do not forget to lubricate the brake fulcrums with the grease-gun, and to coarsen the surfaces of the friction linings when they become glazed through constant use.

Oil on the Brakes. The reader is warned not to let oil drip on to the brake drums or surfaces, or when the brake is wanted in an emergency it will slip until the oil is squeezed or burnt out.

Greasy Roads. On greasy or wet roads, particularly the new by-pass roads, extreme caution should be observed when the brakes are applied, or skidding is almost certain to result, and the speed of the machine should therefore be regulated according to these road conditions. On a greasy road do not apply the brake to one wheel only; both should be applied. Under these circumstances applying the brakes in a series of jabs often has the desired effect, but in any case, whenever the brakes are used, the clutch should be raised so that the braking effort is not applied to the transmission of the engine.

A good driver uses his brakes as little as possible, and the reader is recommended to cultivate the habit of always allowing plenty of space in which to pull up.

Jab Braking. It should be remembered that if the roads are greasy, it is almost an impossibility to pull up suddenly without experiencing skidding. Special care should, therefore, be exercised when driving under these conditions, and the speed of the machine should be reduced when approaching cross roads. The brake should be applied by jabbing, and not with a steady pressure. This prevents the wheel from becoming locked in one position. The jabs should be steadily, not suddenly, applied.

CONCERNING THE TYRES

The pressure to which the tyres are inflated has an important bearing on the questions of comfort, tyre life, braking efficiency, and life of the machine.

" Hard " Tyres. A tyre inflated too hard does not absorb its share of the road shocks set up by potholes, etc., but passes them on to the springs of the front forks. The rider also will be jolted unnecessarily.

" Soft " Tyres. Dealing with the opposite extreme, tyres inflated to too low a pressure soon wear out, because part of the wear is taken by the " wall," or side, of the tyre, which is not meant to come into contact with the road at all. A " soft " tyre may be comfortable from the rider's point of view, but it may allow the rim to come into contact with the road and cause dents.

The Correct Tyre Pressure. The tyres should be inflated to the correct pressure as recommended by the tyre manufacturers, and this pressure should be checked once a week by means of a Schrader pressure gauge. Correct tyre pressure is important to ensure maximum tyre mileage.

Sidecar Alignment and its Effect on Tyres and Steering. Sidecar alignment, if defective, has a bad effect on the tyres and steering, causing the tread to wear on one side. If the tyre is noted to be wearing in this manner, remedy the sidecar alignment and reverse the cover, so that the tyre wear is equalized. See also page 108.

DRIVING A COMBINATION

The actual driving and engine control of a combination does not differ from a solo machine, and the instructions already given need not be repeated here. A solo machine rider will experience a little strangeness with a sidecar outfit, due to the offset drag of the sidecar, which tends to make steering difficult at first by continually edging the machine to the left side of the road and to draw the machine to one side. It is good practice to obtain confidence by taking the machine to the top of a hill and coasting down with free engine, with the foot ready to operate the brake in case of emergency.

The best advice that can be given the new sidecar driver is " go slowly "—particularly on corners. If the rider attempts to take a left-hand turn too rapidly there will be a tendency for the sidecar wheel to rise from the ground owing to the pull of centrifugal force. Once the wheel is off the ground steering control is lost, and the outfit turns to the right, and, in some cases overturns. As the rider gains experience, however, he will find that he can corner faster with safety by adopting the following hints—

Making a Left-hand Turn with Sidecar. Brake before the corner, and then accelerate when actually on the bend. In this way the motor-cycle "runs round" the sidecar, the wheel of which acts as a pivot.

Making a Right-hand Turn with Sidecar. Ride up to the corner fast, and brake when actually on the bend. In this case the sidecar "overruns" the motor-cycle and facilitates the turning action.

After the sidecar has been attached to the motor-cycle for some time, there may be a tendency for the connections to "give" a little, and cause the alignment to be upset. It is advisable, therefore, to check this point from time to time, although the practised combination driver can tell whether the outfit is correctly "lined up" by the manner in which it steers. A pull to the left on an uncambered road is a sure indication that either the machine is leaning inward, or that the sidecar wheel is running outward. Misalignment not only results in bad steering, but it ruins the tyres and imposes undue strains on the motor-cycle frame and the sidecar connections, and, furthermore, reveals the owner to be a man of no mechanical knowledge.

PILLION RIDING

The pillion rider must sit as closely as possible to the driver, and also as "easily" or limply as possible. A good pillion seat and footrests should be fitted to the machine, for the safest method is to ride astride with the feet supported on footrests, and not resting on the backstays nor stuck out. The passenger should sit still, and not lean in either direction, even when rounding corners. Although the machine itself will be "banked," or inclined, when going round a corner, the passenger should endeavour to keep his or her body in the same relation to the machine as when riding on a straight stretch of road. A pillion rider, if sitting astride, should not try to maintain the balance of the machine in traffic, or when taking corners at a low speed, by allowing his feet to touch the ground.

PROCEDURE ON HILLS

Stopping on Hills. A solo machine should always be left with the front wheel pointing *up* the hill, as in this position it cannot "lift" from its stand of its own accord. A combination should also be left in a similar manner, one of the wheels being jammed against the kerbstone or bank and the front wheel turned towards the kerb so that any movement tends to jam the wheel still harder. The low gear should also be engaged.

Starting on Hills. With regard to starting on hills, if the latter are of lesser gradient than one in seven, no difficulty should be encountered if the methods already outlined are adopted. If the hill is steeper, adopt the following procedure : Lift the clutch and apply the brake, the latter operation preventing the machine from running downhill. With the brake on, start the engine, race it a little, and with low gear engaged gradually release the brake, *at the same time gradually letting in the clutch.* This dual action requires practice in order to be carried out effectively, and the beginner may have to start his engine several times until he has acquired the knack.

Starting Downhill. Undoubtedly the best method of starting downhill is to coast down with the clutch disengaged and top gear engaged, until the machine has gathered a fair speed, when the clutch should be slowly engaged.

Braking on Hills. In descending steep hills of appreciable length when the brake would be on for some seconds, use the front and rear brakes alternately, for this prevents the parts of the brake getting very hot.

Using the Engine as a Brake. When descending very steep hills engage low gear at the *top of the hill*, and allow the machine to run down with the throttle closed. On a new machine the novice will probably be astonished at the very powerful braking action this produces. Care must be taken to open the throttle before reaching the bottom of the hill, as otherwise the machine may lose way and pull up unexpectedly. It is not considered good practice to open the exhaust valve when using the engine in this way. The sudden local cooling of certain portions of the engine is liable to cause strains in the material of the cylinder.

RULES OF THE ROAD

After the first two or three spins the reader will find that he has acquired plenty of confidence in the machine, but a word of caution is necessary at this stage, as accidents frequently happen when the driver, in the flush of his newly-acquired control of the machine, feels inclined to throw caution to the wind, forgetting that he has not yet acquired the experience which is sometimes necessary to pull one through an emergency safely.

Drivers' Signals. With every driving licence is issued, by the National Safety First Association, a little booklet which should be studied, for the increased speed and volume of traffic demand that all drivers or riders of vehicles give early and intelligible warning of their intention to make any reduction of speed or

DRIVING

change of course which may affect drivers of other vehicles, and particularly following traffic. Drivers' signals, unlike those given by the police, are simply an indication of the signaller's intention, and do not absolve their giver from first making certain that the projected manoeuvre can be carried out without unduly interfering with others. For example, signalling and turning simultaneously are practically as dangerous as not signalling at all.

Even the overtake signal is merely an indication that, so far as the signaller is concerned, the way on his right is clear for overtaking. But at the same time it is the duty of other road users to act intelligently upon observing all hand signals, and not discourteously to interfere with the projected action.

Whilst superfluous hand-wagging is as exasperating as are redundant road signs, correct hand signals given distinctly, and well in advance, are an essential for safe driving. The wearing of light-coloured gauntlets, particularly at night, make signals more visible. The three officially recommended signals are illustrated in Figs. 16 to 18. The second should be used not only before turning off to the right, but also before swerving or pulling out from the existing traffic line in order to overtake, or to avoid an obstruction. It is equivalent to a warning: " It is dangerous to overtake me on my right." If the signaller is making a complete turn to the right he should, if possible, edge over towards that side so as to leave room on his left for traffic keeping straight ahead. The three signals illustrated, judiciously used and interpreted, give all the vital indications. Until recently there were separate official recommended signals for stopping and turning left, but these have now been discarded.

Various forms of mechanically-operated direction signals are coming into use. As yet they are seldom a satisfactory substitute for the hand signal, and no standards have been officially laid down. Arrows, hands, or pointers usually give the direction, and a red or amber light, or vertical hand or arrow usually indicate " slowing down."

When approaching a traffic controller it is advisable to indicate the direction to take by the signs shown in Fig. 31.

The ordinary turning right signal gives the necessary indication and leaves no room for misunderstanding.

Police Signals. The five standard police signals are illustrated in Figs. 16 to 20. Needless to say, implicit obedience is essential. There is only one occasion when it is permissible to proceed when the constable is holding up traffic (and even then with his consent), and that is when turning left at a cross-road, and when traffic going straight across or turning right is being held up. If the way is clear and the constable's attention be attracted, he will usually indicate that the turn to the left may be made. Extra caution is necessary to avoid danger to pedestrians or vehicles passing across the front.

Unofficial Traffic Controllers. The signals of the uniformed patrols of the motoring organizations should be as rigidly obeyed as those of the police. Danger signals given by ordinary members

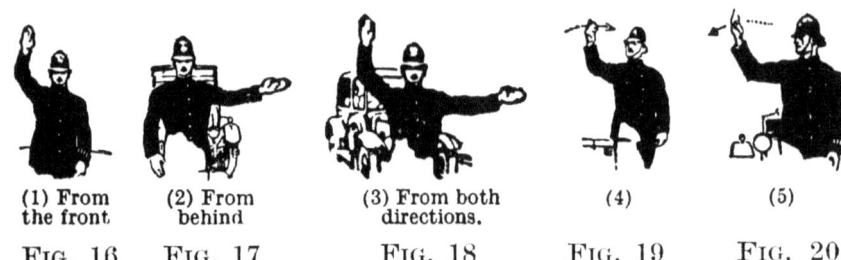

(1) From the front.   (2) From behind.   (3) From both directions.   (4)   (5)

FIG. 16   FIG. 17   FIG. 18   FIG. 19   FIG. 20

FIGS. 16-18. POLICE SIGNALS FOR STOPPING TRAFFIC COMING FROM THE FRONT, FROM BEHIND, OR FROM BOTH DIRECTIONS

FIGS. 19-20. SIGNALS FOR RELEASING TRAFFIC

NOTE. Signals Nos. 1 and 5, or 2 and 5, are also used in combination

of the public should be acted upon, but " all clear " signals from the same source are best ignored.

Road Signs. The familiar red triangle is the standard danger signal, and is usually combined with one of the conventional signs illustrated. In some places a ⊢ or T is used to indicate road junctions other than cross-roads. The warning signs of the responsible road users' organizations have been sited with care, but there are many unwarranted and unofficial notices (e.g. " carriage drive ") which tends to belittle the value of the genuine sign, and which, it is to be hoped, will be done away with under pending legislation. Finger-posts indicate a road junction, and are equivalent to a warning sign. See Figs. 21 to 30.

Other Signs. Other statutory signs are as follows: REDUCED SPEED LIMIT SIGNS. White ring, 18 in. diameter, with plate below (see Fig. 28). It is customary for red bands to be painted on lamp standards, tramway poles, etc., within the reduced speed limit area.

PROHIBITION SIGN. Circular red disc (see Fig. 29).

MOTOR NOTICE. White diamond (see Fig. 30).

White Lines. White guiding lines, when suitably sited, constitute one of the greatest aids to safety on the road. When used

DRIVING 41

to divide up and down traffic on sharp bends all wheels of the vehicle should, as far as possible, be kept to the left of the line. No vehicle should be parked in such fashion as to force other vehicles to cross the line.

Stop lines, running across the near side of the road, are also used to indicate the intersection of a main road—usually with " stop " or " slow " painted on the road. In cities, they are also

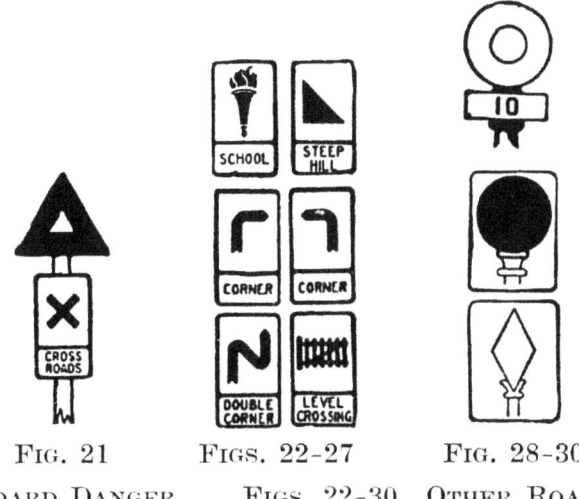

Fig. 21   Figs. 22-27   Fig. 28-30
Standard Danger   Figs. 22-30. Other Road
Signal   Signs

used to hold back traffic at refuges or junctions, to leave room for pedestrians to cross.

Road Junctions. The risk of collision at road intersections is ever increasing. Contrary to common belief, no statutory authority exists giving priority to main road traffic over side road traffic, though custom imposes extra caution on traffic using the less important road.

The Proper Side of the Road. A motorist normally should keep to the left-hand side of the road, except when overtaking another vehicle, when he must pass on the off or right side.

Speed Limit. A speed limit of 20 miles per hour is the maximum speed on the highway where no other speed limit is fixed, although it is proposed shortly to abolish the speed limit; in this respect it is worth pointing out that the offence " driving to the danger of the public," does not necessarily have relation to the speed of the vehicle. You can drive to the danger of the public at 3 m.p.h.

DRIVING IN TRAFFIC

Cross Roads and Corners. Cross roads and corners, perhaps, present the greatest source of danger, and one should always anticipate the presence of a badly-driven vehicle, and pass or negotiate corners at slow speed. When making a turn either to the right or to the left, adopt the scheme shown in Fig. 31, which

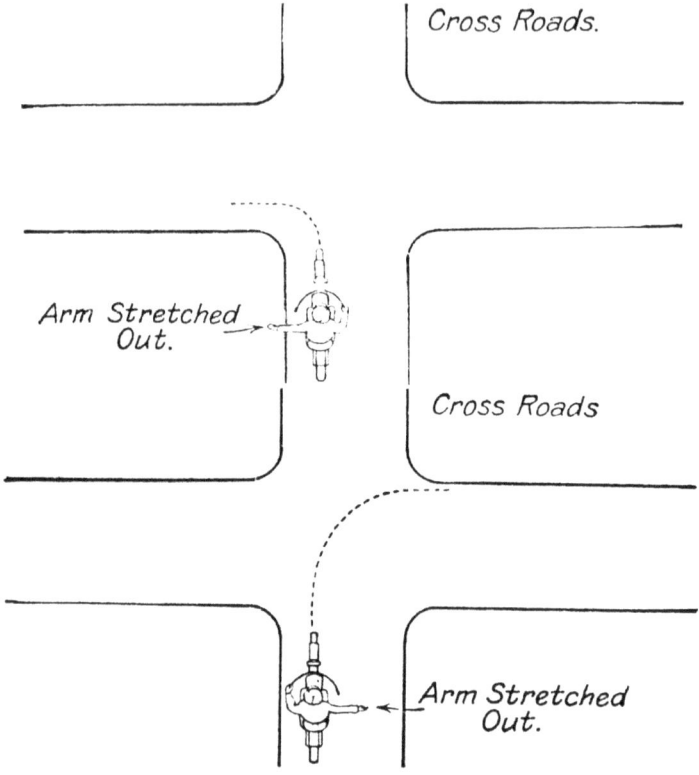

Fig. 31.—How to Warn Following Traffic that you are About to Turn to Left or Right

apprises approaching as well as following traffic of your intentions. The dotted lines indicate the direction that should be taken.

How to Take a Corner. Many expert riders prefer to lean the cycle inward on a curve, and to lean the body in the opposite direction. This is probably the most satisfactory method, but it requires a little practice. The other method is to lean both the cycle and the body inwards.

Stopping in Traffic. To stop in traffic, go into low gear,

DRIVING

declutch, and use the back brake alone, putting the latter only half on for a second or so and then, when the machine is considerably slowed down, putting it on full.

There is no need to stop the engine as some in emergency may be tempted to do, unless the stoppage is likely to be a lengthy one. Keep the clutch disengaged and throttle the engine down until it " ticks " over. If the stoppage is of more than three or four minutes duration, it may be advisable to stop it to prevent it getting overheated.

As a general rule, reserve the front brake for extreme emergencies, when it should be applied at the same time as the back brake.

Warning that you are about to stop should be given as in Fig. 32, and in this respect it is important to remember that the stop should not be too sudden ; you must allow the driver of the vehicle behind you time to interpret your intentions and to pull up, otherwise he may run into your back wheel or you may skid.

FIG. 32.—WARNING FOLLOWING TRAFFIC THAT YOU ARE ABOUT TO STOP

Pottering in Traffic. Sometimes the reader will find that he is compelled to ride in a stream of slow-moving traffic, and he should do this by engaging low gear and closing the throttle till the engine ticks over. Or he may throttle down and use the decompressor, with second gear engaged.

Passing other Traffic. Where the width of the road allows, always pass other vehicles as widely as possible.

Led Horses. A led horse should always be led on the wrong side of the road. It is advisable to give them as wide a berth as possible. They should be passed on the near side.

Passing Tramcars. Tramcars may be passed on either side, but if the offside is clear, it is wise to pass on that side, and that fact would go in one's favour in case of accident. Legally considered, the road is intended for traffic, and loitering, strictly speaking, is illegal.

Tramlines and Skids. Tramlines are dangerous at all times, but wet ones are extremely so. Therefore, if a skid is to be avoided, so should riding on the tramlines, especially if the machine is a solo. When crossing tramlines do so as near as possible at a right-angle. There is then little danger of a skid; but to cross them at a " flat " angle is to ask for trouble.

The same instruction holds good for the stone setts of the centre rail tram system, known as the " underground " system.

Avoiding and Correcting Skids. Skidding is fairly rare if the machine is driven in the manner already outlined. Directly it is felt that the machine is getting into a skid, do not apply the brakes, as this would aggravate the trouble, but lift the clutch, and, if possible, snap the gear lever into the neutral position quickly so that the wheels are free to turn, and then, as the back wheel slides to one side, turn the bars that way, keeping the foot on the footrests, and balance will at once be regained. Get into gear again, let in the clutch and proceed.

A front wheel skid must be placed in a class by itself; it is certainly hard to correct, but it can be done if taken in time by pressing down on that side of the handlebars to which the wheel is slipping and pulling up on the other side.

Traffic Blocks. When a block of traffic can be observed some distance ahead, slow down gradually. The practice sometimes indulged in of approaching it at speed, and suddenly applying the brakes, is not altogether devoid of risk.

The Camber of the Road. Owing to the tendency of heavy vehicles to sideslip when driven on the near side of the road, the drivers of them prefer to drive on the crest. Although this may leave an equal space on either side, it is not advised to pass the vehicle on the wrong side, but to give warning of approach, so that the driver may draw in to enable his vehicle to be passed on the proper side.

Driving Behind a Tram. The short distance in which trams can pull up should be borne in mind when following one of these vehicles, and it is wise always to keep a reasonable distance behind.

Unattended Animals on the Road. Animals, such as horses, cows, pigs, sheep, etc., straying on the roadway represent a real danger, for they do the most stupid things, and when the reader may think an animal is about to leave the roadway and pass on to the grass, it will suddenly dash back into the middle of the road and make passing difficult. It is almost superfluous to tell the reader to stop in such a circumstance and to wait until the animal is well clear, or to drive it away. Do not endeavour to do this by shouting or vigorous operation of the horn; as this may cause even greater confusion.

DRIVING

Modifying Traffic Rules. Safety is the main consideration, and the fact that another may be in the wrong necessitates, perhaps, modifications of the rules. Dogmatically adhering to the law will not save your life when it is endangered by another breaking it, and the doctrine of " doing a great right by doing a little wrong " cannot be altogether ignored. One may thus be compelled to drive the machine on to the footpath in order to avoid a collision.

The Importance of Looking Ahead. A keen look-out ahead avoids tight corners. One may observe over the top of a hedge a horse and cart about to turn into a road on the near side. This enables one to pull up at a safe distance, and the habit of taking a sweeping survey of the view ahead is one to cultivate, and in time becomes second nature. Give ample warning of approach by sounding the horn.

NIGHT RIDING

Almost all of the remarks already given apply to night riding. A red light ahead of course signifies a vehicle either stationary or going in the same direction, and procedure is obvious.

When meeting vehicles going in the opposite direction the glare from headlamps, particularly those of cars, is a source of danger, and although many vehicles are fitted with dimming and dipping devices, this practice is not invariable.

Generally speaking, one should drive at slower speed at night, and a keener look-out is necessary, especially when passing through lanes adjoining fields, owing to the possibility of straying animals.

Courtesy. The great point is to be courteous on the road and considerate to others, thus fostering the friendship and brotherhood of the open road. Bearing in mind the rules given, every road user is urged to consider the safety and comfort of others.

Remember always to—
  Carry your driving licence.
  Keep to the left of the road.
  Go slow past schools and in populous places.
  Overtake on the right, after seeing that the road in front is clear.
  Give warnings with the right arm when slowing down or turning to the off-side.
  Give way whenever possible to traffic approaching from the off-side.
  Pass a led horse on its near side.
  Conform to the lighting and registration regulations.

Recognize warning signs and speed restriction notices.
Realize the discomfort to others of dust and mud splashing.
When going down hill give way to traffic coming up.
Assist the police to regulate traffic by responding promptly to their signals.
Remember never to—
Cut in.
Overtake at cross roads, bends, in narrow village streets, or where an oncoming driver has the right of way.
Abuse the " audible warning of approach."

GENERAL REMARKS

By now the reader will probably be getting to know the sound of his engine. He will, no doubt, have noticed that when the throttle, air and spark are set " just right," the engine purrs along as steadily as can be desired. At other times it may be found that the running is not quite so regular, the engine may seem to thump unduly or there may be mystifying pops or misfires. Each motor-cycle engine has a personality of its own, and will only give of its best to a person who knows its peculiarities thoroughly. Your engine will try and let you know if you are not treating it properly, and if any unusual sound can be detected during running, the good driver will immediately look round to find the cause.

CHAPTER IV

HOW THE ENGINE WORKS

Elements of the Power Unit. There are three main portions of the power unit to be considered—the engine itself, the carburettor, which supplies the engine with the correct mixture of air and petrol gas, and the magneto, whose duty it is to supply a spark at the correct moment to ignite that mixture. These will now be considered.

Types of Engines. Let us deal with the engine first. There are two types into which all motor-cycle engines (and for that matter, motor-car engines) can broadly be classified—the two-stroke and the four-stroke, and in each type there are engines of one, two, or more cylinders. As, however, the number of cylinders does not affect the underlying principle (for an engine with more than one cylinder can be considered as a number of single-cylinder engines coupled together), the purpose of this chapter will be served if only single-cylinder engines are considered. Firstly, then, regarding the four-stroke engine.

THE FOUR-STROKE ENGINE

Elements of the Four-stroke Engine. Fig. 33 shows an ordinary single-cylinder motor-cycle engine as if it had been cut down the centre with a metal saw. It consists of the cylinder, crankcase (to which the cylinder is attached and which carries the bearings for the crankshaft), the piston, connecting rod (secured to the piston by means of the gudgeon-pin), the crankshaft (to which the connecting rod is also secured), the exhaust valve, inlet valve, induction pipe, and sparking plug. The piston is rendered gas-tight by means of piston rings. These rings are introduced to lessen the frictional area, because if the piston itself were made gas-tight in the cylinder, without any rings at all, the friction would be so great that a large amount of power would be lost in overcoming it. Connected to the induction pipe is the carburettor, which is connected by means of a pipe to the petrol tank, and driven from the crankshaft at half the speed of the latter is the magneto, which is connected by insulated wire to the sparking plug.

Principle of the Four-stroke Engine. It has been stated that the engine at present under consideration is known as a " four-stroke."

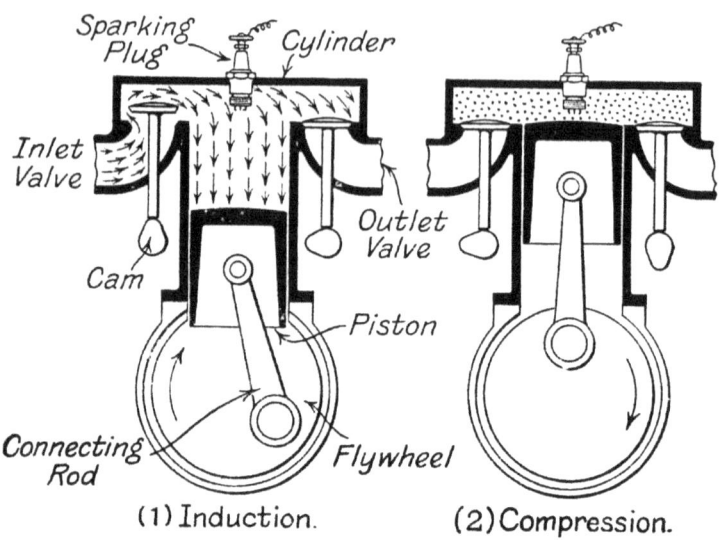
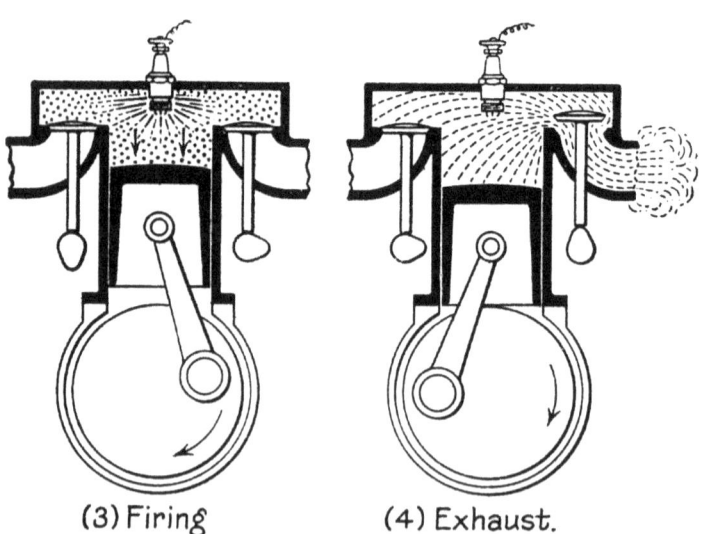

Fig. 33.—The Principle of the Four-Stroke Engine

HOW THE ENGINE WORKS

This is because there are four distinct strokes; firstly, the induction of the charge of petrol-and-air gas into the cylinder; secondly, the compression of that charge; thirdly, the explosion or ignition of it, and, fourthly, the exhausting of the burnt gases. The diagrams (Fig. 33) show the relative positions of piston and crank for these four strokes. Now, how is the charge of petrol gas introduced into the cylinder? When the engine is caused to revolve, the piston exerts a powerful suction on the jet in the carburettor, and (1) the petrol is drawn through the induction pipe into the cylinder through the inlet valve, which is opened to allow the induced charge to pass into the cylinder by means of cams, which push on the valve stems. As soon as the piston reaches the bottom of its stroke, this valve is closed by means of the valve spring, and the piston (2), as it reverses its stroke and travels towards the top of the cylinder, compresses the charge of petrol which is trapped in it. Just before the piston reaches the top of its stroke, a spark occurs at the sparking plug point (only once every four piston strokes, be it noted) and (3) explodes the mixture, forcing the piston to the bottom of the stroke. As soon as it reaches this position, the exhaust cam operates the exhaust valve, which opens to allow the burnt charge to pass into the exhaust pipe, from whence it reaches the atmosphere after passing through the silencer.

The piston now commences to travel towards the top of the cylinder, but this time it does not compress the charge. This stroke is known as the exhaust stroke (4), because its purpose is thoroughly to scavenge the cylinder of the burnt gas. This is pushed out by the piston, and with this object in view the exhaust valve is arranged to remain open during the whole of this stroke, whilst the inlet valve remains closed. When the piston again reaches the top of its stroke, the exhaust valve closes, and the inlet valve commences to open, when the piston again sucks in a charge of petrol from the jet. And so this cycle of operations continues. It will be seen, then, how the four strokes of induction, compression, firing, and exhaust operate.

The Function of the Flywheel. Were it not for the flywheel, the piston could not possibly return to the top of its stroke, and it is the purpose of the flywheel to store up sufficient power from the power stroke to keep the engine running during the strokes of exhaust, induction, and compression.

THE MAGNETO

Its Elements. Briefly, the magneto comprises a permanent magnet with a pair of soft iron pole pieces, which form a tunnel which is magnetically incomplete at the top and bottom, that is,

50 BOOK OF THE B.S.A.

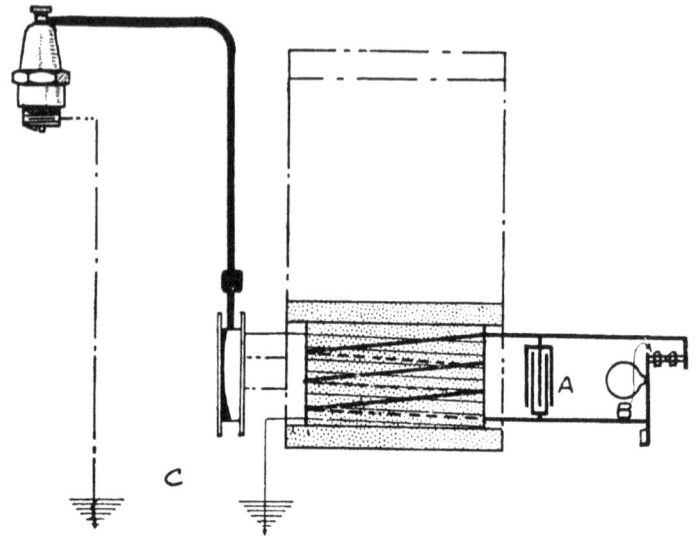

FIG. 34. CIRCUIT DIAGRAM OF MOTOR-CYCLE IGNITION SYSTEM

A. The condenser   *B*. The contact breaker
C. The "earth" (usually the engine)

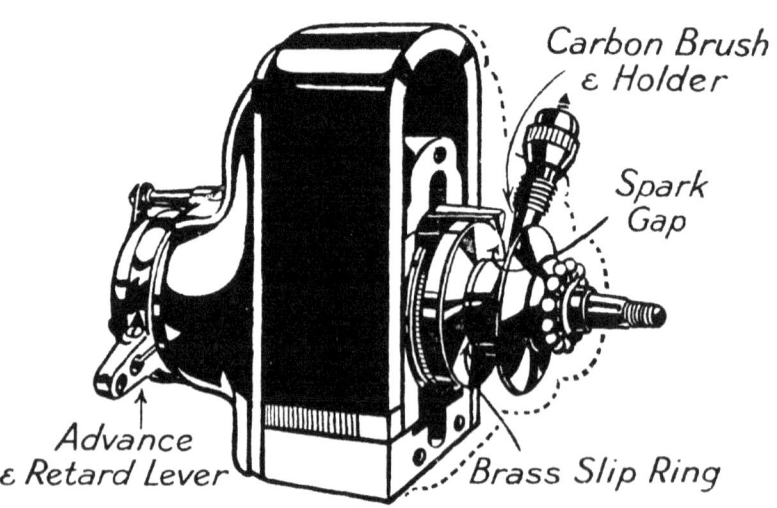

FIG. 35. THE ELEMENTS OF THE MAGNETO

HOW THE ENGINE WORKS

the spaces, for mechanical reasons, are merely filled with non-magnetic metal, such as brass or aluminium (see Figs. 34 and 35). In this tunnel an armature revolves, and this consists of a core built up of soft iron laminations. On this core is first wound a few layers of comparatively thick insulated wire, and the commencing end of this wire is connected to the core, or "earthed," as it is termed. To the outer end of this wire is connected the beginning of another winding, which thus forms an actual continuation of the first, but in this case the wire (which is also

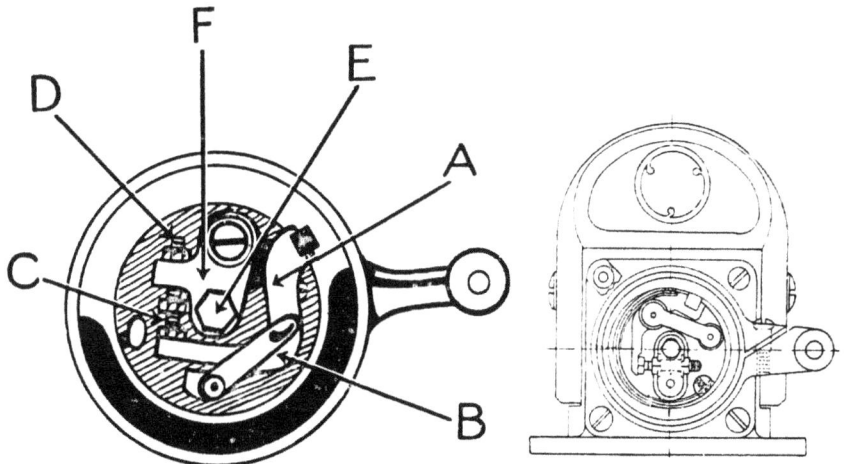

FIG. 36. TWO TYPES OF CONTACT BREAKER

D. Adjustable contact point.   E. Primary pin   F. Insulated block
A. Rocker arm   B. Fibre brush   C. Contact points

insulated) is extremely fine—as fine as a hair, in fact—and is coiled many thousands of times round the core. As it is in this winding that the high-voltage current is generated, it is most carefully insulated from the metal parts of the machine. These two windings are called the primary and secondary, respectively. At one end of the core is mounted a condenser, which is usually enclosed in a brass case, and consists of a number of sheets of tinfoil separated by mica. Beyond this, and mounted on the end of the armature shaft, is the contact breaker.

The Contact Breaker. The contact breaker (Fig. 36) is the switch that breaks the current, and is generally composed of a hinged steel arm, on one end of which is a platinum contact stud, and on the other end a fibre pad which rubs on a cam cut inside the contact-breaker. The platinum stud makes contact with another platinum stud fixed to a plate attached to the armature spindle. The condenser is placed in parallel with the contact-breaker to prevent sparking at the platinum points, and by so doing, conserves the electrical energy that would be wasted in feeding a useless spark. The current generated reaches its maximum intensity when the armature is at the position where its pole-faces are at the top and bottom (as shown in Fig. 37). As the armature comes into this position twice per revolution, it will be seen that it should be possible to obtain two sparks per revolution, and this is done in the case of a magneto for a twin-cylinder engine. Where a single-cylinder machine is required, only one cam is fitted in the contact breaker, and thus the current is broken only once per revolution and one spark is allowed to run to waste.

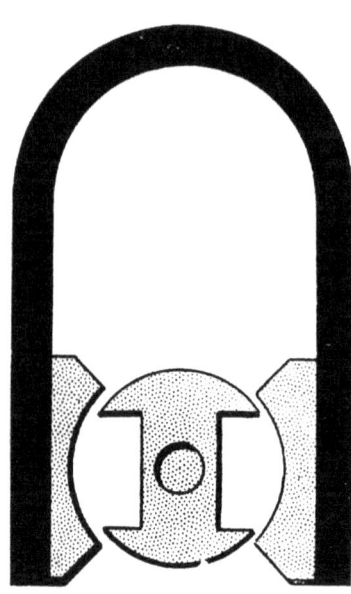

FIG. 37. THE CURRENT IS AT A MAXIMUM WHEN THE ARMATURE IS IN THE POSITION SHOWN HERE

Single-cylinder Ignition. As the single-cylinder magneto produces one spark per revolution, and in the case of a four-stroke only one spark is needed every two revolutions of the engine, the magneto is driven at half-engine speed; while in the case of a two-stroke single-cylinder engine the magneto runs at engine speed. Twin four-stroke magnetos are also geared to run at half-engine speed, while two-stroke magnetos run at double this pace. One end of the secondary wire is attached to the primary and the other connected to a brass slip ring, against which is pressed a carbon pencil to which is connected the wire that feeds the sparking plug.

The Armature. The armature is mounted on a pair of ball races which are lubricated when the machine leaves the factory, and they therefore require but little attention. The ends of modern magnetos are provided with aluminium cover plates into which are let felt strips that assist in making the machine practically watertight. On the side of the contact-breaker cover is a lever, connected by Bowden wire to a control on the handlebar. The operation of this causes the contact-breaker cover to move through a small arc of some 30°. As the cam is cut on the inside of this cover, a 30° movement allows of an alteration of timing by

HOW THE ENGINE WORKS 53

that amount and provides one with an advanced firing position for fast running, and a retarded one for easy starting. As, however, the further the spark is retarded the further it recedes from its maximum efficiency position, the range of advance is limited to 30°. This is one of the very few inherent disadvantages of a very reliable and useful device.

THE CARBURETTOR

Primary Functions. The primary function of a carburettor is to supply a combustible mixture to the engine. To do this the

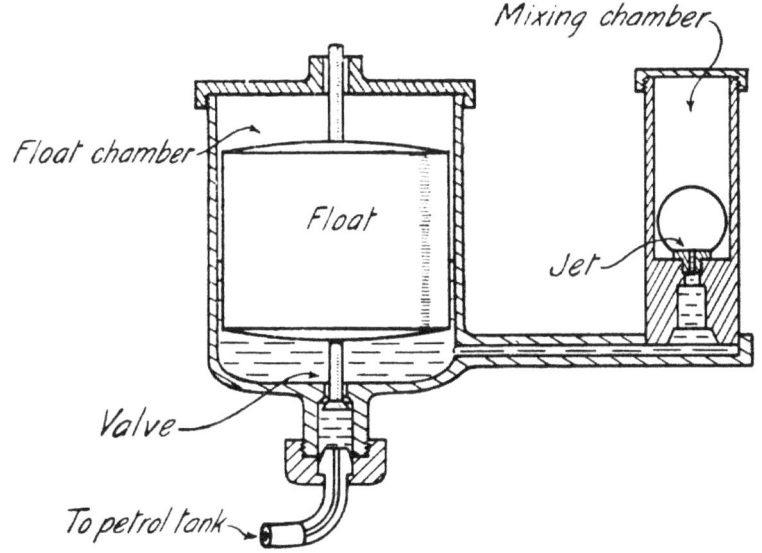

FIG. 38. DIAGRAMMATIC REPRESENTATION OF CARBURETTOR

carburettor has to measure the quantity of air passing, simultaneously measuring the corresponding amount of liquid petrol, and add the petrol to the air in the form of a fine spray, so that the petrol may vaporize readily. Figs. 38 and 39 show sections of the carburettor and its choke tube respectively.

Mixture Strength. The mixture strength should be about 14 parts, by weight, of air to 1 part of petrol for best results. An engine will run on a mixture as rich as 8 to 1, but would not develop full power, and the petrol consumption would be very heavy, as a lot of the petrol would pass out via the exhaust, incompletely burnt; on the other hand, an engine will run with a mixture as weak as 20 to 1.

The Jet. To measure the minute quantity of petrol required for each power stroke by mechanical means, such as a microscopic pump, for instance, would require extremely delicate apparatus, but fortunately it can be done much more simply by means of a tiny hole, known as the jet. The size of the petrol jet is very important; a little alteration, not noticeable to the eye, will make a lot of difference in the performance of the engine.

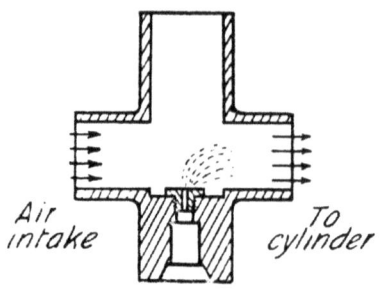

Fig. 39. Diagram showing how the Airflow "Sucks" Petrol from the Jet

The Pressure Over the Jet. Besides the actual size of the jet, the pressure producing the flow has to be reckoned with. Obviously, there would be no flow of petrol through the jet unless the pressure on the surface inside the float chamber was greater than the pressure at the top of the jet. A flow could be obtained by increasing the pressure in the float chamber, but it is much easier to reduce the pressure in the region of the jet orifice by means of a venturi tube. This is generally referred to in connection with

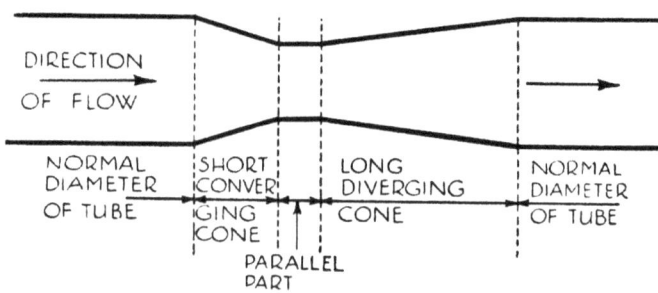

Fig. 40. The Venturi Tube is Merely a Tube of the Form Shown Above

carburettors as a "choke" tube. The venturi is merely a tube of varying diameter, as shown in Fig. 40.

At first the tube converges somewhat gently to a smaller diameter, then there is usually a short parallel portion of the reduced diameter, after which the tube diverges very gradually to its original diameter. It is essential that the changes in diameter should occur gradually without any abrupt changes of section to cause eddying currents.

Jet Arrangement. The jet is arranged at the throat of the venturi, where the pressure is lowest. The petrol in the float chamber being subject to full atmospheric pressure, the petrol spurts out of the jet and is broken up into a more or less fine spray. The increased air velocity by the venturi, therefore, serves the double purpose of creating a reduction of pressure, which

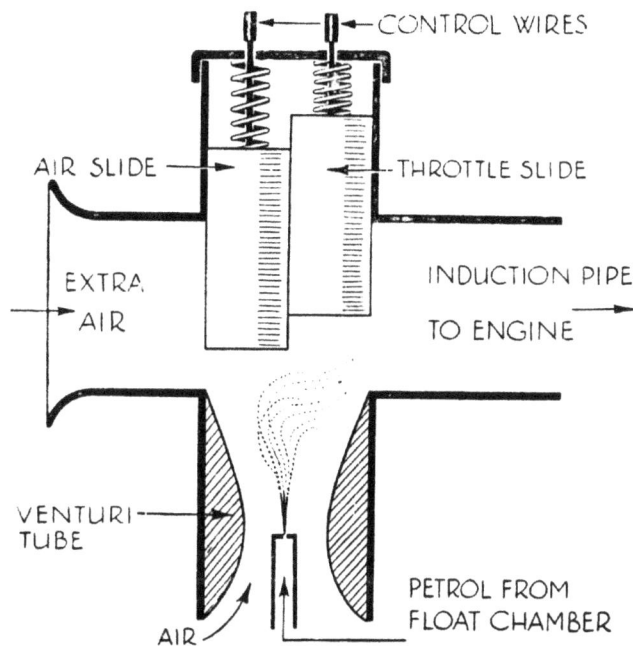

FIG. 41. A TYPICAL ARRANGEMENT OF A VENTURI-TYPE MOTOR-CYCLE CARBURETTOR

makes the petrol flow from the jet, and at the same time breaks up the stream of petrol into a spray.

Weakening the Mixture. A very small venturi tube is used in order to give a good suction on the jet when the throttle is nearly shut, and at full throttle, when the mixture would be too rich, it is diluted to normal strength by large quantities of extra air (see Fig. 41). This arrangement requires only one jet, and the mixture strength is adjusted by the rider to suit the conditions of the moment. He adjusts the levers to give better running; the mixture strength will not be far out if the engine runs properly.

The single-jet carburettor is, of course, easy to adjust compared with the multi-jet one, but, after the initial adjustment, the latter needs no continual " taptwiddling " attention from the driver. Some motor-cycle carburettors have no venturi at all, while in

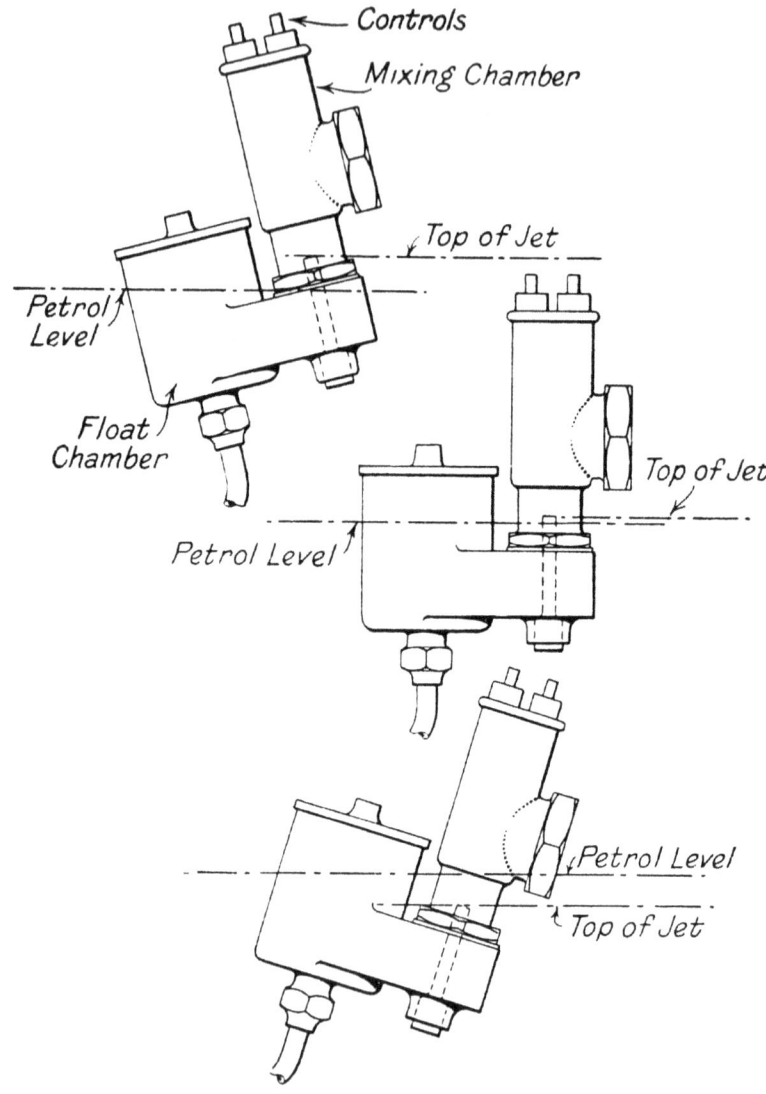

Fig. 42.—Diagram showing Relation between Petrol Level and Jet, and showing how Inclining the Machine Alters the Petrol Level

HOW THE ENGINE WORKS

some modern instruments the air intake and the induction pipe connection are formed into the shape of a venturi, with the controls at the throat providing a straight-through path for the air.

The Float and the Float Chamber. Motor-cycle carburettor float chambers are of two types—top feed and bottom feed. In the first the petrol flows from the tank to the float chamber via a pipe secured to the top of it, and in the latter the petrol enters through the bottom of the float chamber.

Inside the float chamber is a float, to which is attached a needle having a tapered end. As the petrol enters the float chamber the float, carrying the tapered needle, rises " or floats," until the tapered end of the needle closes the inlet orifice. As the engine sucks in the petrol from the float chamber via the jet, the float sinks slightly, and as the needle sinks and uncovers the petrol inlet, a fresh supply of petrol is admitted. Obviously, without a float the petrol would merely spurt out through the jet.

The Advance and Retard. The advance and retard lever is fixed to the left side of the handlebars and causes the spark to occur about $\frac{1}{4}$ in. before top dead centre in the fully advanced, and about $\frac{1}{16}$ in. *after* top dead centre in the fully retarded position. Most engines have a " best " position for these levers, which can only be found by trial.

THE TWO-STROKE PRINCIPLE

How the Two-Stroke Works. The two-stroke engine is simpler in operation than the four-stroke, the fundamental principles of which have already been explained. We saw that a four-stroke engine is so named because it has one power or firing stroke in every four strokes of the piston, or in other words, in every two revolutions of the crankshaft. For a similar reason the two-stroke is so named, because it has a firing stroke for every revolution of the crankshaft which, of course, means every two strokes of the piston. Its action is simple and, because of that, remarkable; in spite of the fact that it has no valve mechanism properly so called, the functions of induction, compression, explosion and exhaust are carried out with much less expenditure of power. Because the number of working parts is considerably fewer, the type is ideal for the beginner, and the four diagrams on the next page will help the reader to understand its cycle of operations. The first illustration shows the piston at the top of its stroke with the charge of petrol-and-air gas fully compressed and on the point of being ignited. The arrows indicate that the upward stroke of the piston has induced or sucked-in a charge of gas

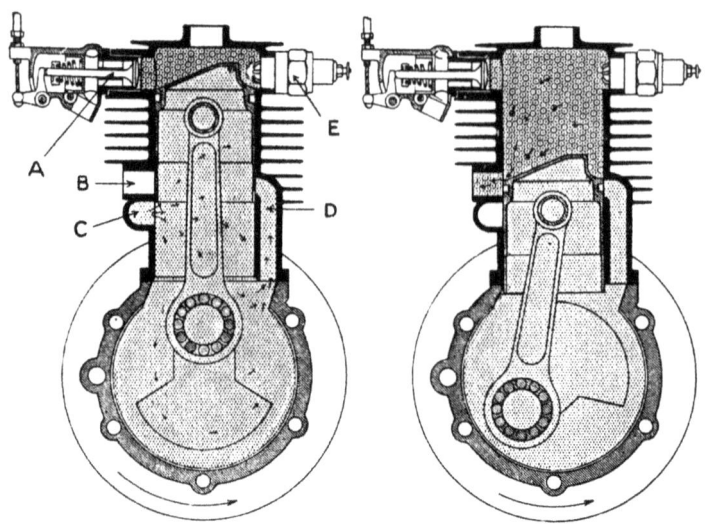

Fig. 43.—Inlet Port Open, Admitting Gas to Crankcase. Exhaust and Transfer Ports Closed

Fig. 45.—Exhaust Port Just Opening. Fresh Charge Compressed in Crankcase

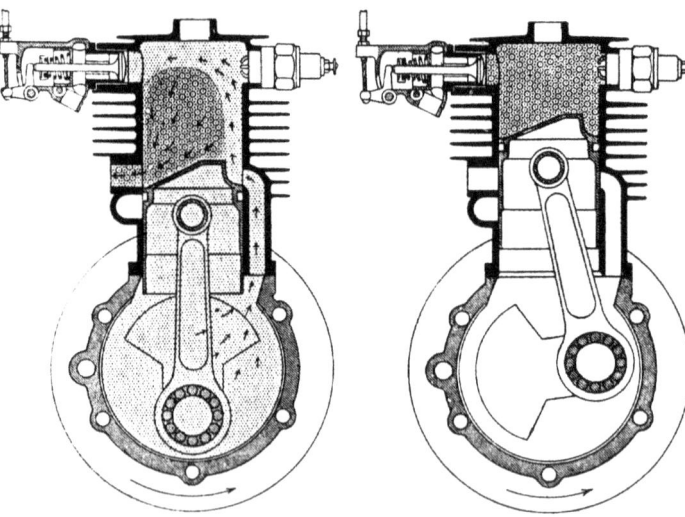

Fig. 44.—Exhaust and Transfer Ports Fully Open

Fig. 46.—Fresh Charge Transferred from Crankcase to Combustion Chamber. Piston on the Up-stroke

[In these four diagrams, A is the compression release valve, B the exhaust port, C the inlet from the carburettor, D the transfer passage and port, and E the sparking plug.]

HOW THE ENGINE WORKS

from the carburettor through the inlet port C (Fig. 43), so that whilst the piston is on its up-stroke compressing the charge above the piston, it simultaneously draws into the crankcase the mixture for the next charge. The ignition of the charge, of course, forces the piston down to the bottom of its stroke, and the condition of affairs is then as is shown in Fig. 44. It will be noticed that the exhaust port is uncovered before the piston uncovers the transfer port, thus enabling the bulk of the burnt gas to be expelled before the fresh charge enters the combustion chamber. The gas, thus trapped in the crankcase, is forced by the down-stroke of the piston via the transfer port into the cylinder head at the same moment as the burnt charge passes out via the exhaust port. In Fig. 45 the down-stroke is completed, and the arrows indicate the direction of flow of the gas. The dotted portion in the combustion chamber represents the exhaust gas. In Fig. 46 the up-stroke is commenced, and the cycle of operations as here explained is repeated. It will be noticed that the piston is specially shaped at the head to direct the flow of the exhaust gas and the fresh charge, so that they are separated. Unfortunately, however, a small proportion of the fresh charge passes out with the exhaust, because both inlet and exhaust ports are open for a moment at the same time.

It will, of course, be clear to the reader that, as a power stroke commences every time the piston of a two-stroke is approaching top dead centre, a spark must be made to occur at every revolution of the crank. This differs from the four-stroke, which, as we have seen, only requires a spark at every fourth piston stroke. For this reason the magneto is driven at engine speed.

It will be obvious that absolute gas-tightness in all parts of the engine is important to its successful functioning. The piston and rings must be a good fit to prevent leakage between the crankcase and the combustion chamber, crankcase joints and bearings must be gas-tight, and the transfer and exhaust ports must be kept scrupulously clean.

But the fact that there is so little to go wrong with the two-stroke renders it particularly suitable for the beginner. Its torque is, of course, very much more even than a single-cylinder four-stroke engine and, as a matter of fact, is almost equal to that of a twin-cylinder engine.

CHAPTER V

MECHANICAL DETAILS OF THE B.S.A.

THE beginner is usually too enthusiastic and anxious to ride his machine to bother his head about its constructional details. Sufficient for him that the machine runs. There comes the time, however, when he begins to ponder over such matters, especially when overhaul becomes necessary, or when adjustment necessitates dismantling some part of the machine. A knowledge of

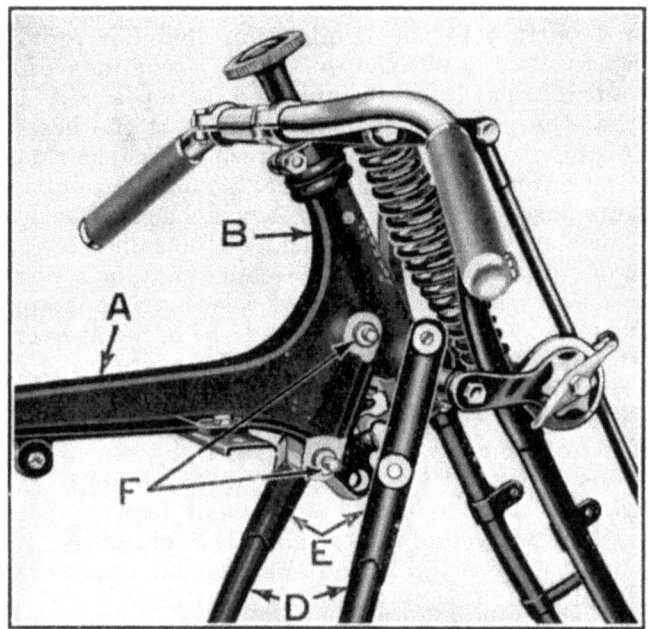

FIG. 47. THE HEAD ARRANGEMENT

the construction at such times is valuable, for it enables him to do the particular job much more quickly than he would if he had to fumble about to find out how the various parts were secured.

When studying the machine it is easier to follow out the assembly if the parts are considered as units, and study should be directed to each unit as if the rest of the machine did not exist.

Frame. The frame of all the inclined engine models has been re-designed. The general outline and duplex cradle construction

MECHANICAL DETAILS OF THE B.S.A.

have been retained, and in its latest form it possesses immense strength without excessive weight. Instead of the tubular top member joined to the short tank rail a single high-tensile steel forging A (Figs. 47 and 48) is used, emboding the head lug B at the front end and the seat lug C at the rear, forged in one piece. The usual brazed joints at the ends and at the centre are thus eliminated, and a much stronger and more reliable construction is obtained. This gives the machine a backbone of forged steel and means greater strength, safety, and comfort.

The forging is of a wide I section which is gradually increased from rear to front in such a way that it offers uniform resistance to bending throughout its length. At the front, immediately behind the head lug, where the vertical loading on the top member is high, a very deep section is employed. This forging is also designed to withstand the side and twisting strains which occur during fast or heavy sidecar work, and to provide a degree of rigidity which results in complete stability on grease and on rough surfaces. The duplex down tubes D (Figs. 47 and 48) are brazed into separate forgings E, which are bolted to the head lug and located on substantial registers F, two of these being provided for each tube. At their lower ends the front down tubes are reinforced and trapped. They are then joined to the front chainstay ends G by means of registers through which the front engine bolt passes. The seat tubes H, which are also duplex, are securely bolted to the seat lug and engine gear-box cradle plates. Each of the chainstays extends as a continuous member to the front, where it unites with one of the front down tubes. The duplex construction of these members prevents frame distortion due to the heavy chain tension which occurs at high speeds, which is liable to absorb power and to cause transmission noise and rapid wear of chains and sprockets.

THE ENGINE

Parts of the Engine. We have already seen how the petrol engine works, and the elements of the engine (piston, crank, etc.) were explained at the time. It may, then, fairly be supposed that the reader will not require further reference to this matter.

No detailed mention has yet been made of "side-valve" engines or "overhead-valve" engines.

The Side-valve Engine. In the early forms of motor-cycles, what is known as superposed valves were used. That is to say, the inlet valve was placed immediately over the exhaust valve. The inlet valve usually was automatically operated by suction, which caused it to lift on the induction stroke and admit the

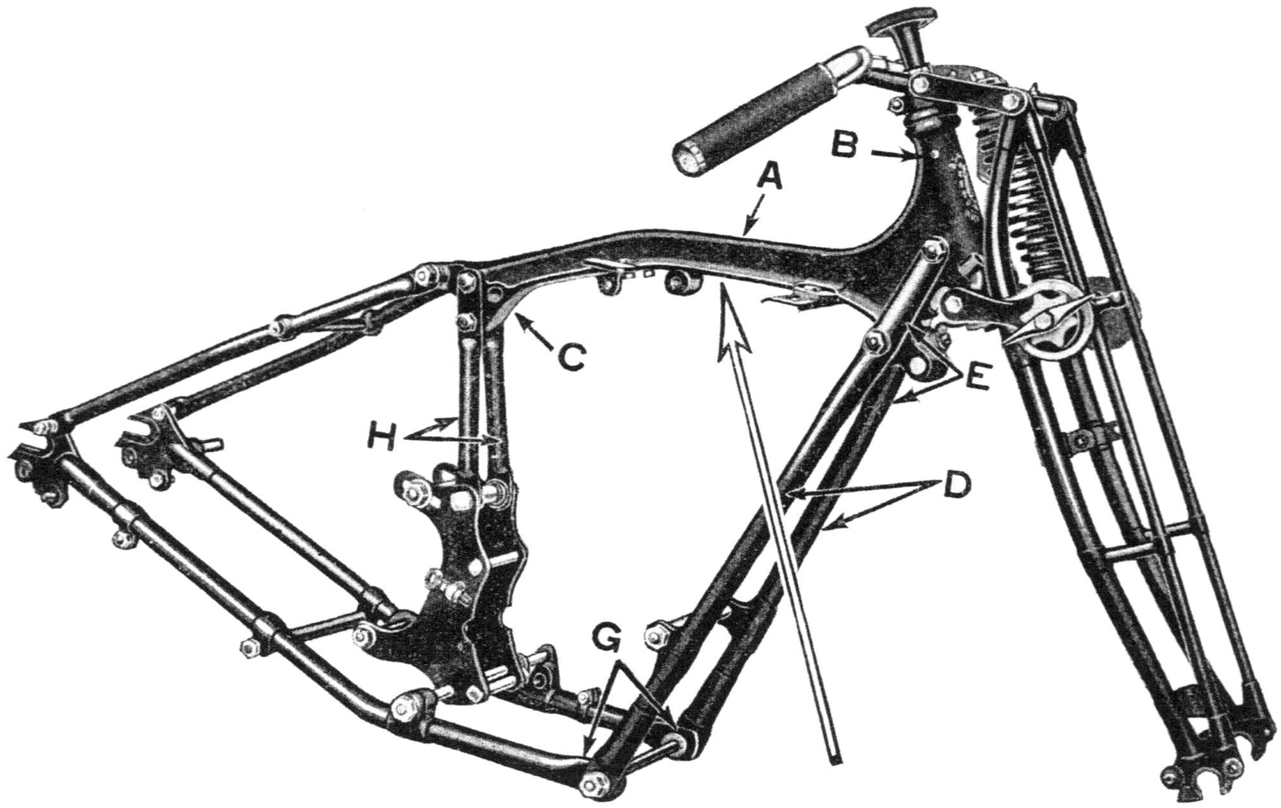

FIG 48. DETAILS OF FRAME CONSTRUCTION

MECHANICAL DETAILS OF THE B.S.A. 63

charge of petrol-and-air gas. Automatic valves, however, were so troublesome that mechanically-operated valves were introduced (the honour of introduction belongs to the Minerva Co.), and instead of the valves being superposed, they were placed side by side. It will be seen that the inlet valve, as well as the exhaust valve, is mechanically operated. By far the majority of cars and motor cycles now have this valve arrangement. Mechanically-operated overhead valves are in use to-day on almost all well-known makes of motor-cycles.

The Overhead-valve Engine. Even as side-by-side valves were an improvement on superposed valves, so (theoretically, at any rate) are overhead valves an improvement on side-by-side valves. The advantages claimed for it are that a more perfect design of cylinder is possible, and that better carburation is obtainable as the turbulence (the swirling motion) of the gas, so necessary to efficient carburation, is greatly improved. Two types of overhead-valve gear are in use to-day, one carried by a detachable cylinder head, and the other in a detachable seating. An engine fitted with overhead valves is more speedy than a similar model with side valves, and, judging from present tendencies, overhead valves will be universal in a few years' time.

Inclined Engine Features. An outstanding feature of all B.S.A. motor-cycles is the generous size of all wearing parts to ensure long life with minimum attention. The alloy steel connecting rod A (Fig. 49) is scientifically designed to give strength with lightness. It transmits the surge of power to the crankpin B which is drilled with an oil passage C. A continuous current of lubricant is pumped under pressure to the double row big-end bearing D. Tapers in the forged steel flywheels grip the crankpin and the whole assembly rotates in the generous bearings. At E the mainshaft is housed in both ball and roller bearings' at F in a roller bearing (ball bearing on side valve models), and at G the oil feed is arranged. So the sprocket H runs in perfect precision, giving a noiseless chain drive.

The patented design of valve gear gives up to 1,000 miles at high speed without the need to set the valve clearance. The scientific springing scheme ensures that the valve follows the cam contour up to 5,400 revolutions per minute—45 perfectly timed openings and closings a second. And all this with commendably quiet operation due to well-proportioned wearing surfaces. The timing pinion I, with wide working face, drives the cam wheels J separately. The cam wheels, on fixed shafts with central oil supply, operate circular flat base tappets L. The regular rotation of these presents changing contact lines to the cam action, with consequent long life.

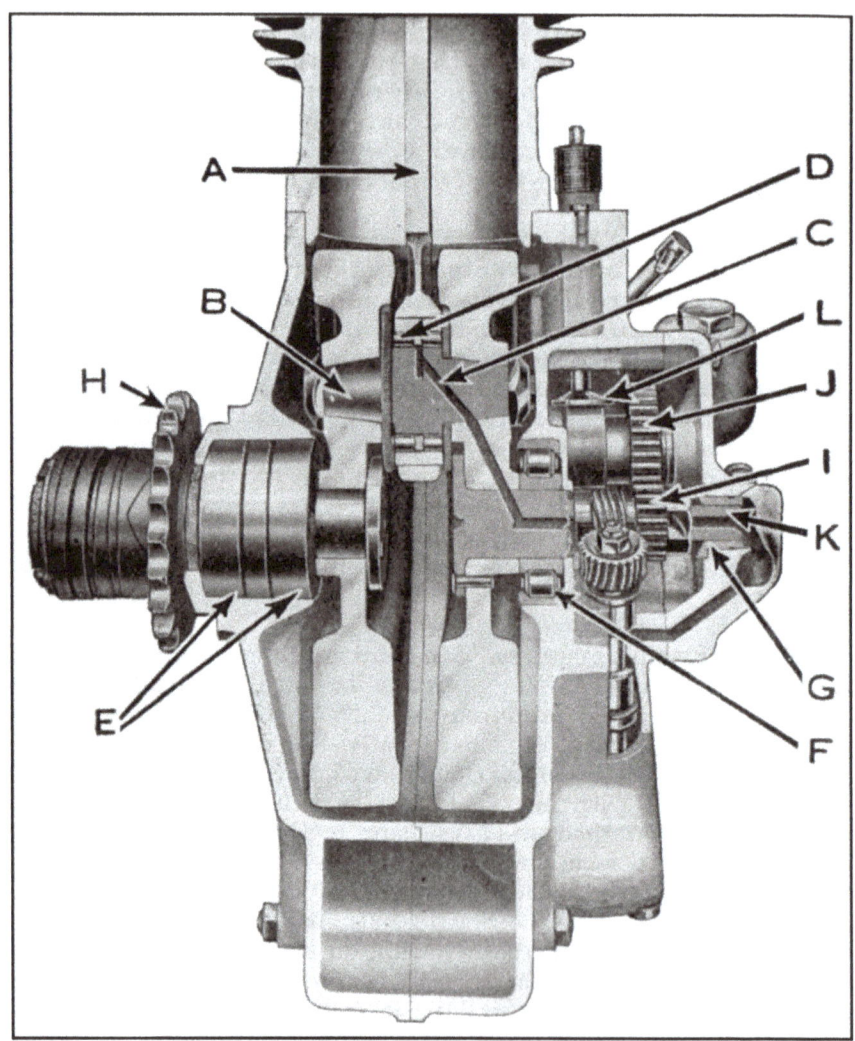

Fig. 49. Showing Engine Features

THE CUSH DRIVE

Purpose of the Cush Drive. The purpose of a cush (short for " cushion ") drive is to eliminate the harshness which accompanies the use of chain drive, and it certainly tends to reduce wear on the back tyre, and enables the power from the engine to

MECHANICAL DETAILS OF THE B.S.A.

be " picked up " gradually. With the now out-of-date belt-driven machine (or chain-and-belt) the cush drive was unnecessary, for the flexibility of the belt served the same purpose. In actual practice the friction clutch itself is a cush drive, for it slips a little when " picking up."

A cush drive of the spring-loaded cam-face type is mounted on the engine mainshaft of all models except the 1·74 h.p. Any

FIG. 50.—THE CAM-FACED CUSH DRIVE (WITH COVER REMOVED) AS FITTED TO 4·93 H.P. LIGHT SIDE-VALVE MODEL

irregularities in the driving torque of the engine cause the driving member to recede from the sprocket against spring pressure, and so rotate slightly without driving the sprocket. This ensures an extremely smooth drive. It is automatically lubricated by oil mist from the crankcase.

New Pattern Cam-cush Drive. In the present range of B.S.A. models the cush drive somewhat resembles the ratchet mechanism of a keyless watch. In this later pattern, one large coil spring connects the engine with the countershaft, the connection between the spring mounting and the engine shaft being in

66 BOOK OF THE B.S.A.

the form of a cam-faced serrated plate, but capable of a little give and take on either side. This is illustrated in Fig. 50.

The Two-speed Gear Fitted to the 1·74 h.p. Model. The two-speed gear, fitted to this model up to 1929, which is combined

Fig. 51.—Cush Drive Dismantled

Fig. 52.—The B.S.A. Fork Links

Fig. 53.—Internal View of the Internal Expanding Brakes

with the engine unit, is of the constant mesh type. Gear changing is effected by sliding the dog clutch A (Fig. 59) engaging the dog clutch B for high gear and the dog clutch C for low gear. In the intermediate position the gears are in neutral, i.e. the engine is disconnected from the rear wheel. The dog clutch moves from one position to another by means of operating fork D (mounted on the control shaft E) engaging in a groove in the dog clutch. The peg F on the control shaft, working in a helical cam slot in the fork, converts the rotary movement of the outside gear lever

MECHANICAL DETAILS OF THE B.S.A.

G into a sliding motion of the operating fork. A spring-control plunger registering in notches in the quadrant plate *H* (Fig. 59) gives definite location to the gears.

The efficiency and life of the gear will be greatly increased if the following instructions regarding lubrication are carefully adhered to. Unscrew the cap from the oil filling spout on the rear of the box and fill with B.S.A. heavy gear oil until no more

FIG. 54.—THE ALUMINIUM PISTON

Note the Gudgeon-Pin Fixing
There are now no oil grooves in the skirt.

can be poured in after working the kick-starter once or twice. If you cannot obtain this oil use Castrol D, Mobiloil C, or Shell gear oil. Another suitable lubricant is Speedwell " Crimsangere Light " mixed with a small quantity of B.S.A. engine oil. If the machine is in regular use this level should be maintained by frequent filling. After every 1,000 miles' running thoroughly flush the box with paraffin. Top gear should be engaged and the kick-starter operated several times (with the clutch out) to circulate the paraffin. Then carefully drain out the paraffin and the oil through the drain plug, which is situated underneath it at the left-hand side, and fill the box to the correct level with fresh oil. From 1929 a three-speed gear-box is fitted, the two-speed being discontinued. It is shown in Fig. 55.

The Three-speed Countershaft Gear. This gear-box, although similar in principle to that which is fitted to the heavier machines, is smaller and more compact. The three-speed gear-box fitted to the 3·49 h.p. and the 4·93 h.p. models is, like the two-speed gear-box, of the countershaft type, with all pinions in constant mesh, and an external clutch of the dry-plate variety.

The Dog Clutch. The changing of gears is effected by sliding dog clutches *A* and *B* (Fig. 57), and the method by which the dog clutches are given the necessary movement constitutes one of the principal features of the device.

On the shaft *C* (Fig. 57), which is rotated by means of the pinion

Fig. 55. The Gears of the 1·74 h.p. Two-stroke Model

Sliding dog-clutch A, operating fork E, control shaft F, control shaft peg G, quadrant plate H

and quadrant *D*, which is operated by the lever at the side of the tank, are mounted two operating forks *E* and *F*, the arms of which engage in the grooves of the dog clutches *A* and *B*. Helical cam grooves are formed in these forks, which engage pegs *G* fixed in shaft *C*. When the shaft *C* is revolved by means of the operating mechanism, the pegs *G* cause the forks *E* and *F* to slide along, the cams being cut so as to give the required position to the sliding dog clutches, *A* and *B*.

The Low Gear. When the low gear is put into operation, the dog clutch *B* is moved into engagement with pinion *J*. The drive is transmitted by means of central shaft *H* and pinion *I* to pinion *J*, then through dog clutch *B* to shaft *K* and pinion *L*, which in turn drives pinion *M*, to which the rear chain sprocket *N* is attached.

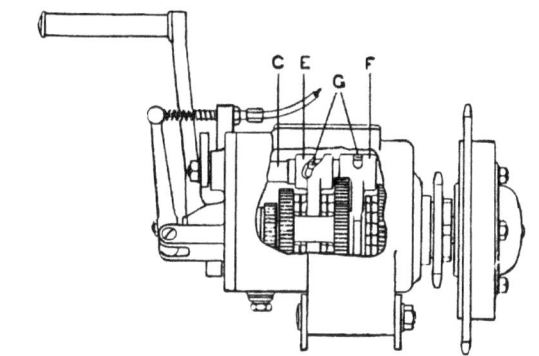

Fig. 56.—Three-speed Gear-box (Outside View)

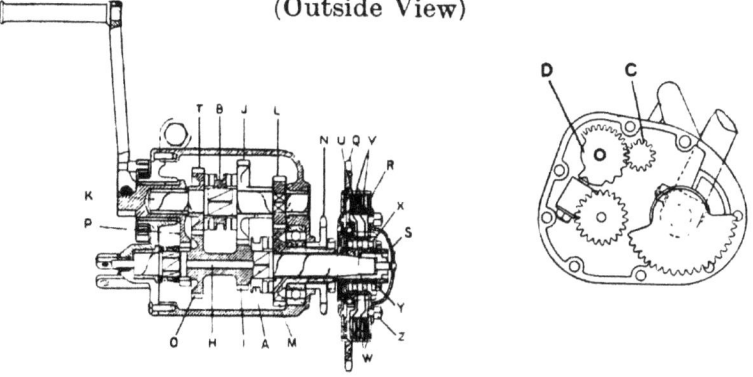

Fig. 57.—Three-speed Gear-box (Inside View)

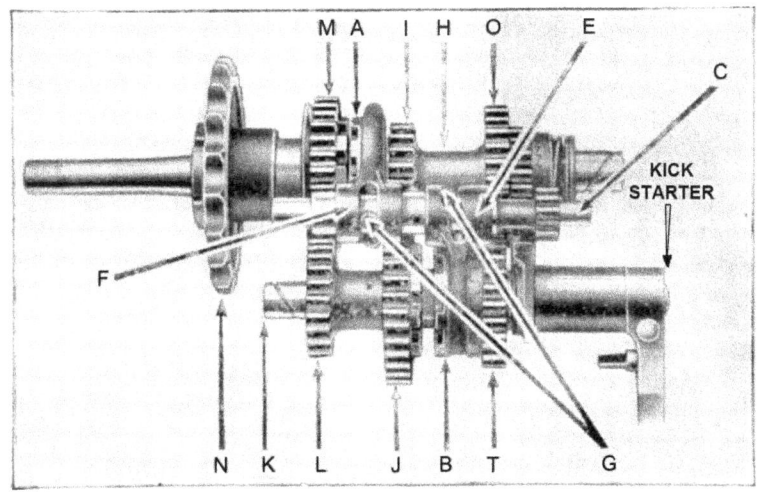

Fig. 58.—An Internal View of the Gear-box, with the Clutch Removed

The Second Gear. The second gear is obtained by rotating shaft C, which withdraws dog clutch B from engagement with pinion J into engagement with pinion T. The drive is then transmitted from shaft H through pinions O and T, then, as previously, through pinion L to pinion M and rear chain sprocket.

The High Gear. The high or normal gear is effected by a further rotating of shaft C, which withdraws dog clutch B from

Fig. 59.—The Two-speed Gear Integral with the Engine as Fitted to the 1·74 h.p. Two-stroke up to 1929

pinion T, and engages dog clutch A with pinion M, clutch B being retained in an inoperative position. Pinion sleeve M, with sprocket N, is thus coupled direct to shaft H, pinions J, T, and L revolving idly. When changing up from low to high gear it is imperative that the drive of the engine should be disengaged momentarily by releasing the clutch.

Engagement of Dog Clutches. A novel means of ensuring correct position of all gears is arranged in the gear-box operating mechanism. The quadrant D is formed with teeth round part of its circumference only. On the plain portion of the periphery a number of pockets are provided, which engage with a spring plunger mounted on the boss of the gear-box cover. The spring plunger on change lever is thus dispensed with.

MECHANICAL DETAILS OF THE B.S.A. 71

Starting the Engine. To start the engine, the gear lever is moved to the neutral position. Each dog clutch is now out of engagement. Movement of the kick-starter crank rotates quadrant P mounted on shaft K, which in turn engages with ratchet pinion mounted on shaft H. In order that its engagement shall be certain, without jamming, the first tooth in quadrant P is of special form. All difficulty of engagement is thus obviated. On the road, the engine can be started by means of the kick-starter only when the gear is in " neutral " position.

Position of Clutch when Starting. The clutch is left in to start the engine, the gear lever being in the neutral position. When the engine has been started, the clutch is withdrawn by a lever on the left of handlebar, and the low gear is then engaged by moving operating lever to the low gear position. The clutch can then be engaged, when it will be found that the load can be taken up in a particularly smooth and efficient manner.

General Procedure when Changing Gear. When changing gear this procedure should be followed: If the clutch is eased slightly when changing down from high gear to second, or second to low, the shock of engagement is reduced. Assuming high gear to be in operation, to change to second gear the lever should be pushed forward smartly to the stop in the midway position, and to change to low gear the lever should be moved slightly to the right to clear stop in gate, then being pushed smartly forward.

As already stated, the three-speed gear-box fitted to the 5·57, 7·70, and 9·86 h.p. models differs only in point of size and not in principle.

THE CLUTCH

The Clutch. This is of the floating dry-plate type. On the larger models it consists of seven friction rings and eight steel plates arranged alternately. There are thus fourteen bearing surfaces with a total area of more than 200 sq. in.—an unusually large area for a motor-cycle clutch (Fig. 60). Every second steel plate is coupled by splines to the clutch drive which is driven by the primary chain. The other steel plates are splined to the clutch sleeve which is keyed on to the gear-box mainshaft. There are six clutch springs, and when the clutch is engaged these force the steel plates and friction rings together in such a way that the entire assembly rotates as a solid mass transmitting power from the engine shaft to the gear-box mainshaft. The large bearing area and effective diameter of the plates permit of the use of medium strength springs. The clutch is, therefore, light to handle

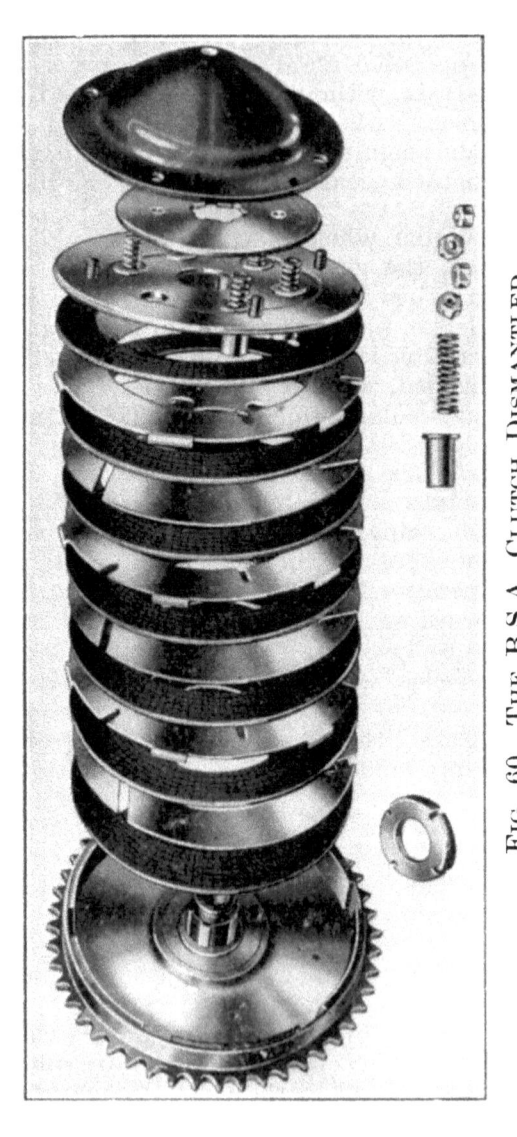

FIG. 60. THE B.S.A. CLUTCH DISMANTLED

and sweet in engagement, and it possesses that delicacy of control which contributes so largely to the pleasure of driving. In the smaller models a lighter clutch of similar construction is fitted.

FIG. 61.—THE B.S.A. PLATE CLUTCH

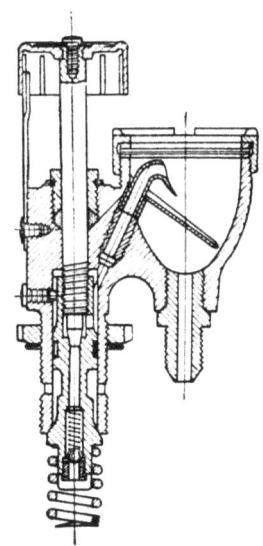

FIG. 62.—CROSS-SECTION OF THE OIL PUMP

The clutch is provided to enable the driver to " disconnect " the drive from the engine to the gear-box when desired, and to enable the power from the engine to be gradually taken up. The half-tone (Fig. 61) in conjunction with the details given in the paragraph on the countershaft gear, makes further explanation unnecessary.

74   BOOK OF THE B.S.A.

Note the order in which the plates *U*, *V* and *W* are arranged, so that they can be assembled in the same order. (See Figs. 90 and 91.)

THE LUBRICATION SYSTEM

The 174 c.c. Two-stroke Lubricating System. The lubrication system of the two-stroke is the simple and efficient one of mixing the oil with the petrol (known as the Petroil System). The great advantage of this system is that it does undoubtedly proportion the oil used to the amount of work done. A mixture of the correct proportions is conveniently prepared if the measure combined with the petrol filling cap is used. After the tank has been nearly filled with petrol, three of this measure full of oil should be poured into it. The tank can then be completely filled with petrol. If preferred, the petrol may be prepared before filling the tank by adding $\frac{1}{2}$ pint (the filling cap measure is exactly $\frac{1}{4}$ pint) of oil to a gallon of petrol.

Lubricating System of 7·70 h.p. and 9·86 h.p. Models. With the 7·70 h.p. and 9·86 h.p. models the lubrication system is by gravity feed to mechanical pump, then to sight feed on the tank, feeding to the crankcase. A hand pump is also fitted for emergency use. Oil is supplied to the front chain by depressing a spring by-pass valve on the timing case. A mechanical pump is mounted on the timing cover; it is of the eccentric type, and is of ample capacity to meet all possible requirements. The oil is fed to the pump by suction and gravity through a pipe underneath the tank on the right-hand side. The pump, which is driven from the inlet cam, consists of a spindle having a groove formed round part of its circumference into which falls a spring-loaded plunger. When the leading edge of the plunger leaves the groove, oil is sucked in through the inlet pipe. The groove in the spindle is now filled with oil, and on further rotation comes again into contact with the plunger, which forces the oil along a second pipe up to the sight feed situated on the tank and thence to the engine. The lower end of the delivery pipe from the sight feed to the engine enters a distributor of special design situated on the crankcase between the cylinders, which ensures an equal supply to both cylinders and pistons.

The lubrication system for the 4·93 h.p. S.V. and O.H.V. Light is as follows. The oil is fed by gravity from the tank to the mechanical pump, which consists of a worm operating in a fixed sleeve in the timing gear cover. Incorporated in the same unit is a tap, which controls the supply from the tank to the pump, and a special sight feed and control knob. There are three positions of the tap. When it is pointing towards the cylinder

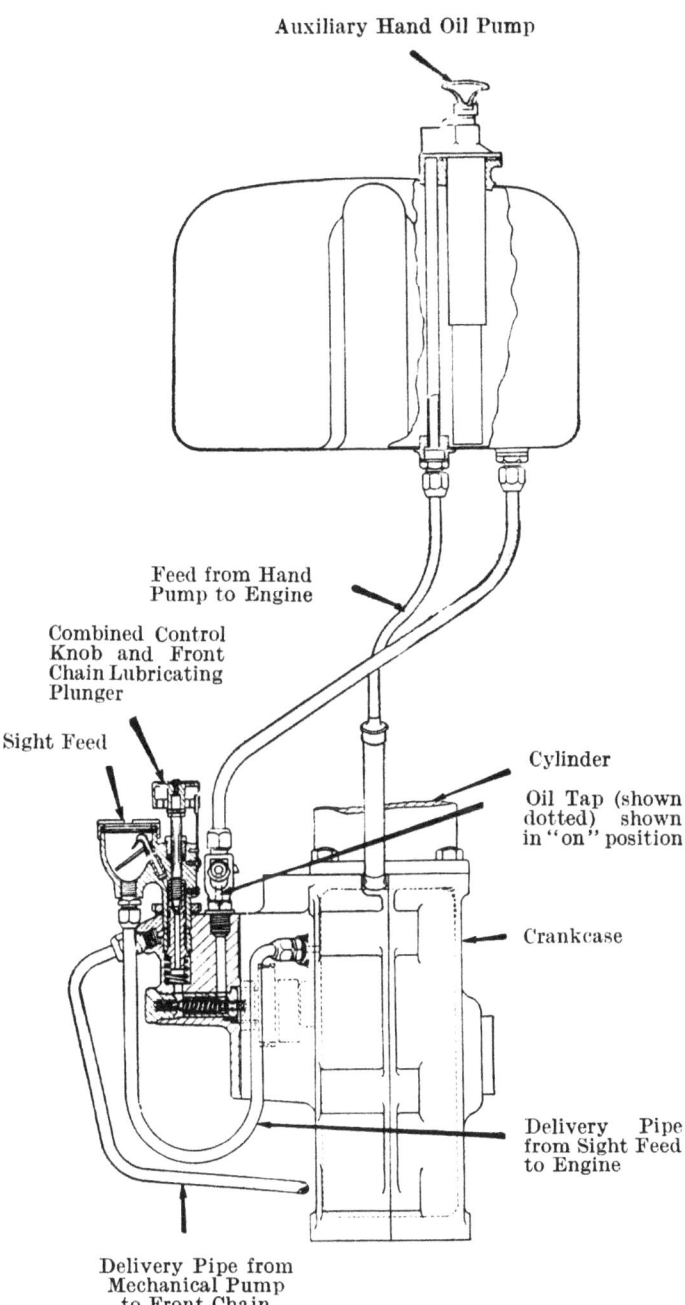

Fig. 63. The 4·93 h.p. S.V. Light Lubricating System

the oil supply to the pump is cut off, and when the tap is turned vertically downwards oil is supplied to the pump. In the third

Fig. 64.—Detail View of 4·93 h.p. Light Side-valve Cylinder, showing Exhaust Valve Lifter

or "test" position the tap points horizontally away from the engine, and oil is discharged through a small spout fitted to the side of the tap. This arrangement is useful for determining whether the oil supply is in order or not. When the tap is turned on (i.e. downwards) oil is delivered by the pump through the

MECHANICAL DETAILS OF THE B.S.A.

control valve into the sight feed chamber, which it enters through a spout. It then falls in the form of drops into a special trough

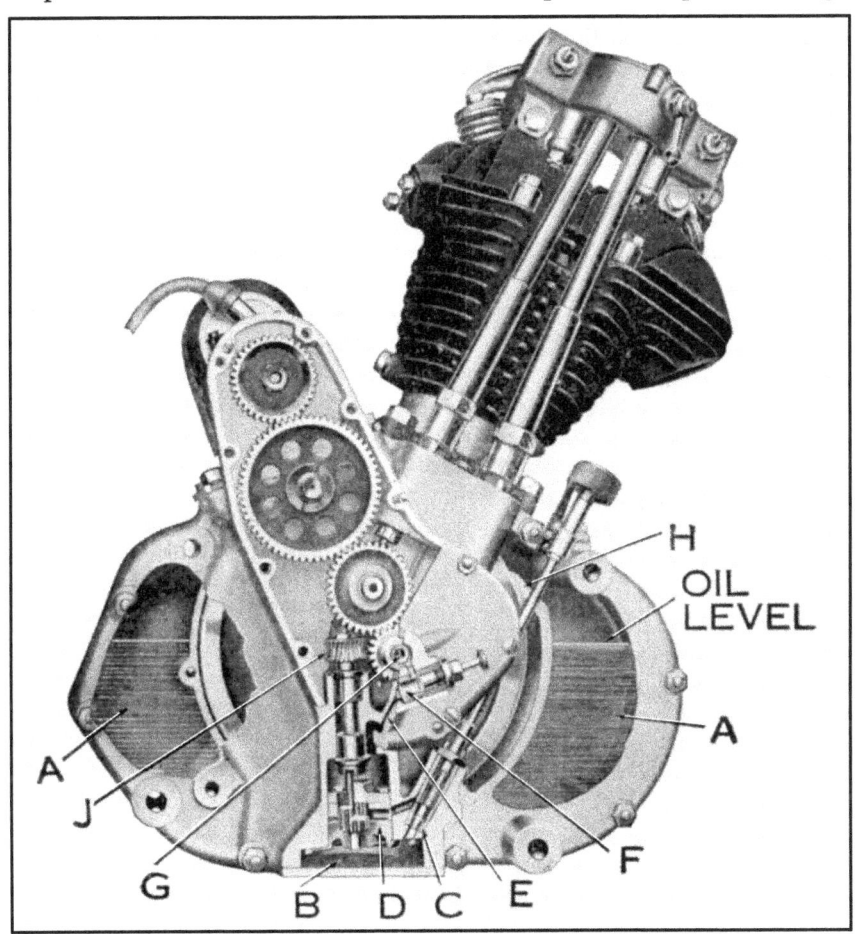

FIG. 65.—THE OIL SUMP IN DETAIL

fitted underneath the spout, arranged to be easily seen by the rider.

GENERAL LUBRICATION SYSTEM APPLICABLE TO MOST MODELS

Sump Lubrication on Inclined Engine Models. The lubrication system of all the inclined engine models is designed on car lubrication principles, and is a vast improvement over the old type of mechanical oil pump. It cuts out all external oil pipes, which are liable to break or become stopped up, and ensures greater efficiency in the lubrication of the most vital part of the engine—the big-end bearing. The big-end bearings of B.S.A. models equipped with a circulating sump lubrication receive 250 times as much oil as the big-ends in engines fitted with the ordinary system, yet the oil consumption is remarkably economical.

The oil is contained in the double sump A (Fig. 65), passes through the reservoir B, and past the adjustment valve control C

Fig. 66. View of the 2·49 h.p. Oil Sump

to the pump D. It is then driven up the passage E into the tell-tale chamber F, forces out the tell-tale plunger, enters the hollow crankshaft G, and so through holes drilled in the flywheel and crankshaft to the big-end bearing. After cooling and lubricating this bearing, the oil is thrown on to the cylinder walls and the underside of the piston. It returns to the crankcase and is picked up and carried round by the flywheels. The scraper H returns it to the sump. The pump is driven by worm gear J from the main shaft, and being submerged, is always full of oil and cannot fail to operate. Once the correct setting for the control knob is obtained you need never touch it again. So long as you replenish

MECHANICAL DETAILS OF THE B.S.A.

the sump every few hundred miles the pump will faithfully provide perfect lubrication.

Sump Lubrication on Lightweight Models. On all of the lightweight models the lubricating system is similar in principle to the sump lubrication on the inclined engine models, differing only in detail. The oil is contained in the sump *A* (Fig. 66), passes through the filter *B*, up the hole *C* to the pump, forcing out the tell-tale plunger on its way. The pump delivers oil past the adjustable control valve, and through the hollow mainshaft and holes drilled in the flywheel and crankpin to the big-end bearing. A portion of the oil is diverted to the timing and mainshaft bearing. After cooling and lubricating this bearing the oil is thrown on to the cylinder walls and the underside of the piston. It returns to the crankcase and is picked up and carried round by the flywheels. The scraper *D* returns it to the sump.

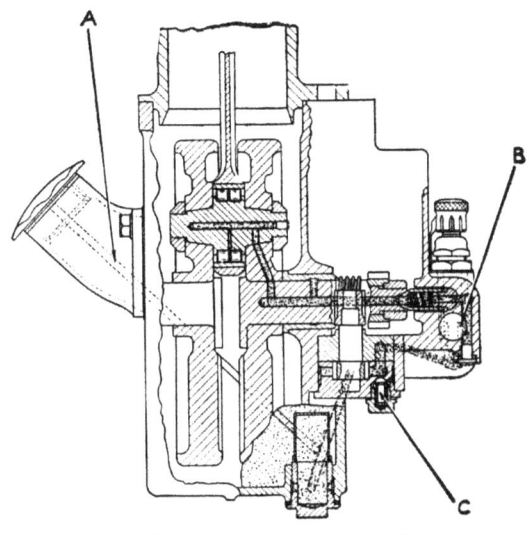

FIG. 67. SECTION SHOWING OIL-FEED IN BIG-END DRY SUMP LUBRICATION SYSTEM

An automatic release valve between the pump and control valve regulates the oil pressure in accordance with the control valve setting. Once the correct setting for the control knob is obtained you need not touch it again. So long as you replenish the sump every few hundred miles the pump will faithfully provide perfect lubrication.

The Lubricating System Described in Detail. Cast integral with the crankcase is a sump the capacity of which is $2\frac{1}{2}$ pints. The gear-type pump, driven by skew-gearing from the timing-side mainshaft, rotates at one-sixth engine speed and delivers filtered oil to the big-end bearing through passages cut in the crankcase, timing-cover, mainshaft, flywheel, and crankpin. The oil enters the annular space between the two rows of rollers and the centre portion of the phosphor-bronze cage. A portion of the oil from the pump is pressure-fed to the timing-side mainshaft bearing (see Fig. 07).

After lubricating the big-end the oil reaches the other parts of the engine by splash. Any excess of oil is picked up by the flywheel rims from the bottom of the crankcase and is removed by a scraper acting on the flywheels and returned to the sump. The oil supply is controlled by a valve on the delivery side of the pump. The valve is easily accessible to the rider from the saddle.

On the intake side of the pump a tell-tale is fitted. This takes the form of a small spring plunger (B, Fig. 68), which is forced outwards by the passage of oil mounted on the timing-cover and

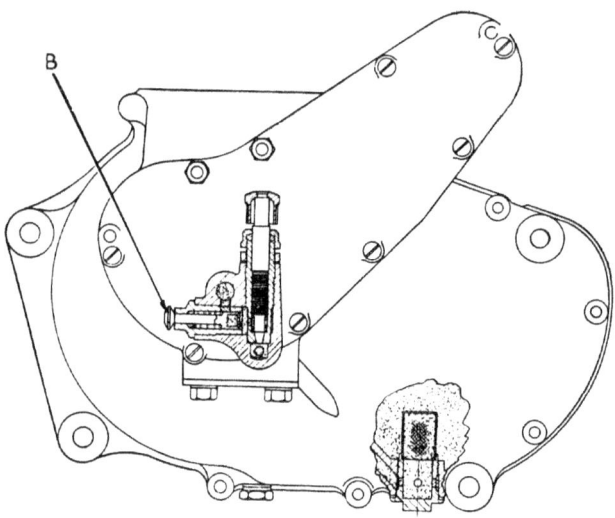

FIG. 68. DRY SUMP LUBRICATION SYSTEM

visible from the saddle. So long, therefore, as the pump is working the tell-tale projects. An automatic release valve (C, Fig. 67) is arranged between the pump and the control valve. This regulates the oil pressure in accordance with the control valve setting.

An oil lever dipper-gauge (A, Fig. 67) is attached to the sump filler cap. This consists of a rod which projects within the sump, reaching to the bottom. The rod is of D-section, and on the flat side pint graduations are marked. To test the oil level in the sump it is only necessary to remove the dipper by unscrewing the sump filler cap and examining it. If the oil level on the dipper-gauge is indistinct, wipe it clean, reinsert, and withdraw it again. It will then be very clearly marked. The filler is mounted at the side of the sump in such a position that oil can be filled up to the correct level but not above it. It is provided with

MECHANICAL DETAILS OF THE B.S.A.

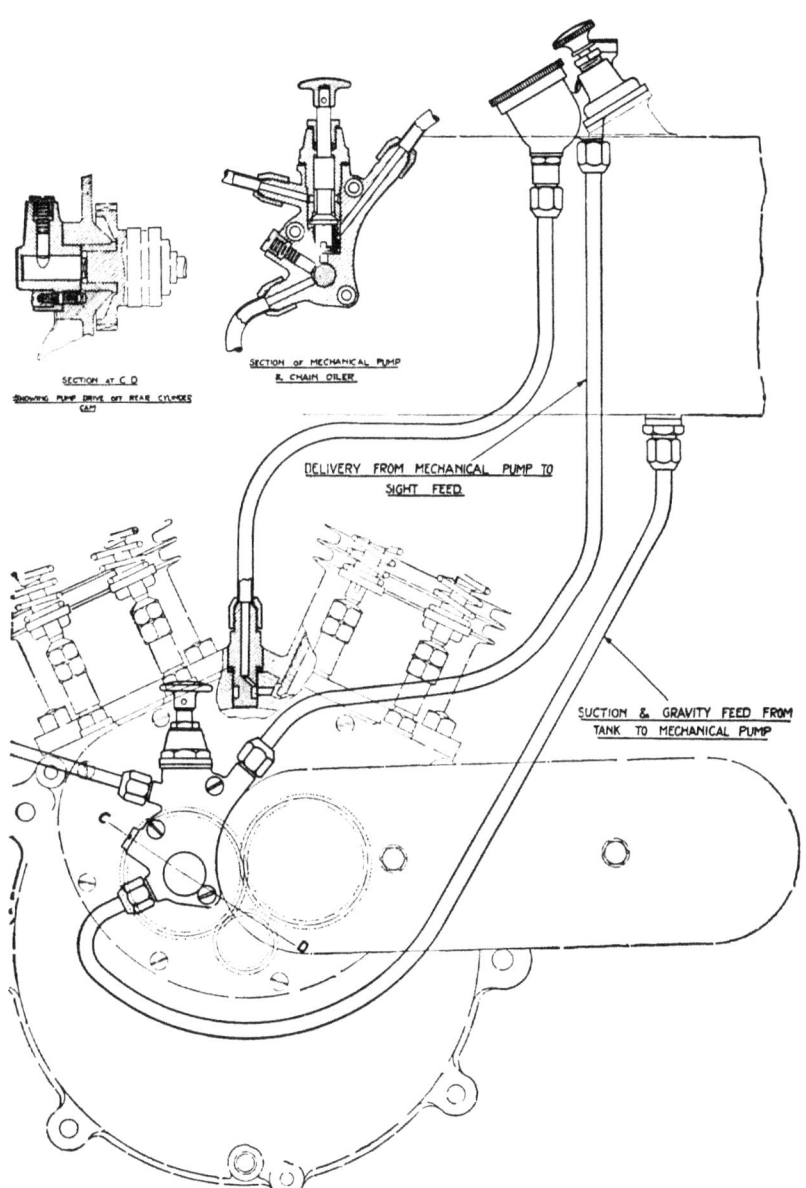

Fig. 69.—The Lubrication System of the 7·70 h.p. and 9·86 h.p. B.S.A. Models

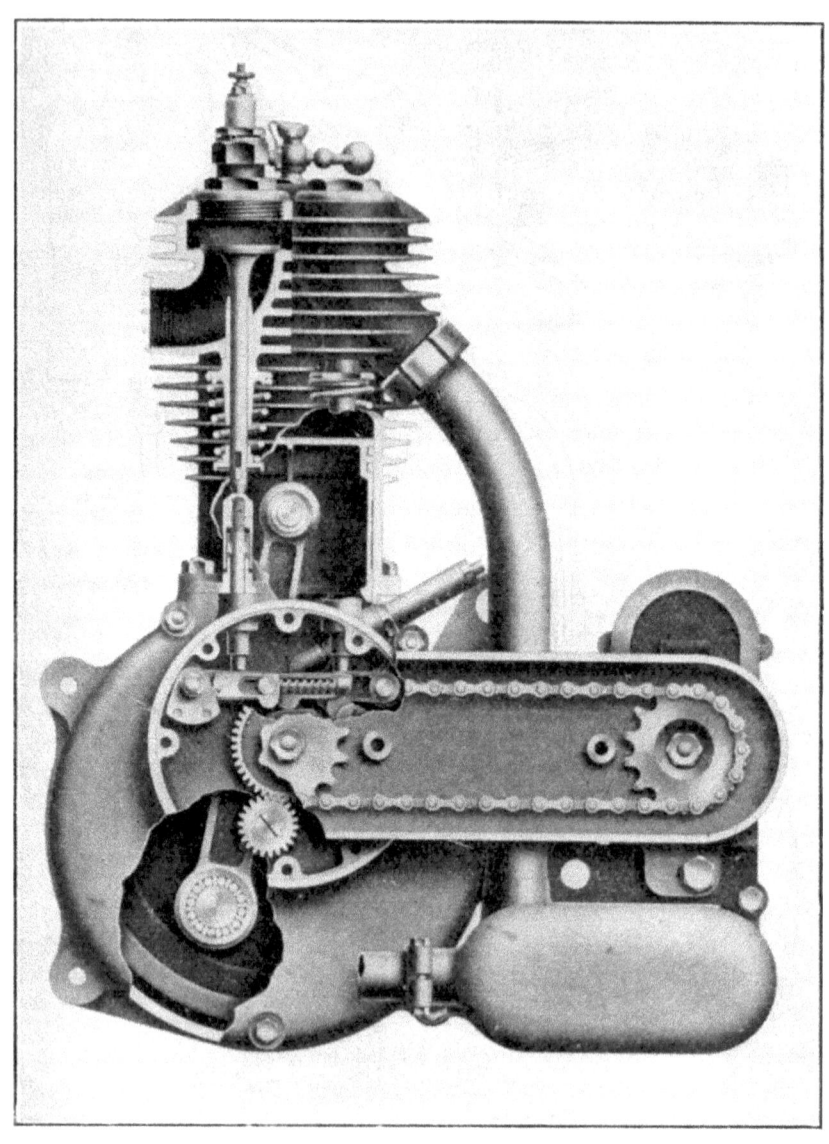

Fig. 70.—Cut-away Detail View of the 5·57 h.p. (1921) Engine, showing Timing Gear

MECHANICAL DETAILS OF THE B.S.A.

a cap which can be tightened by hand without the use of a spanner.

Lubrication is arranged for the engine shaft cush-drive by oil mist passing from the crankcase through a hole in the mainshaft. A special oiling device for the front chain consists of a small reservoir formed on the inner near-side crankcase wall. Oil accumulates in this and passes through an adjustable valve, accessible to the rider, and thence through a special hollow stud placed so that oil emerging from it drips on to the front chain.

Instructions for Lubrication. For ordinary running the oil pump control valve should be opened (turned to the left) from half to three-quarters of a turn. This setting is only arbitrary, and the rider should find out for himself the most economical setting consistent with adequate lubrication. The tell-tale provides the best guide for correct oil control setting. If it projects about $\frac{1}{4}$ in. the setting is about correct. If it moves out farther than this the setting should be reduced. If the tell-tale moves in and out continuously instead of remaining stationary, it is a sign that the engine is not receiving sufficient oil due to the control not being far enough open or to the sump becoming empty. These instructions apply for normal touring speeds. If the machine is consistently driven at high speeds the setting should be increased slightly. When the engine is new the oil supply should be fairly generous for the first 500 miles. The engine should be given about 25 per cent more oil than the above settings indicate.

Attention should be paid to the following points in connection with the lubricating systems: Check the oil level in the sump regularly by means of the dipper (A, Fig. 67). When the level falls to the notch marked "$\frac{1}{2}$" the sump should be filled up with $\frac{1}{2}$ pint of oil. If preferred, the sump can be filled up with $1\frac{1}{2}$ pints of oil when the level falls to the mark "$1\frac{1}{2}$" on the dipper. It is of the utmost importance, however, not to run more than about 20 miles after the oil level has fallen to the mark "$1\frac{1}{2}$." If this distance is exceeded engine trouble may occur due to lack of lubrication.

When the engine stops firing the tell-tale should be gradually drawn in under spring pressure. If it remains out this may be due to the presence of grit or dust on the stem, and the latter should be cleaned with a piece of rag. If a very heavy oil is used it may be necessary to push the tell-tale home with the fingers.

THE SILENCER

The noise of the exhaust gas is reduced by allowing it to expand before it is expelled into the air, this expansion taking place in

Fig. 71. Lubrication Diagram for B.S.A. 2·49 h.p. and 3·49 h.p. Motor-cycles

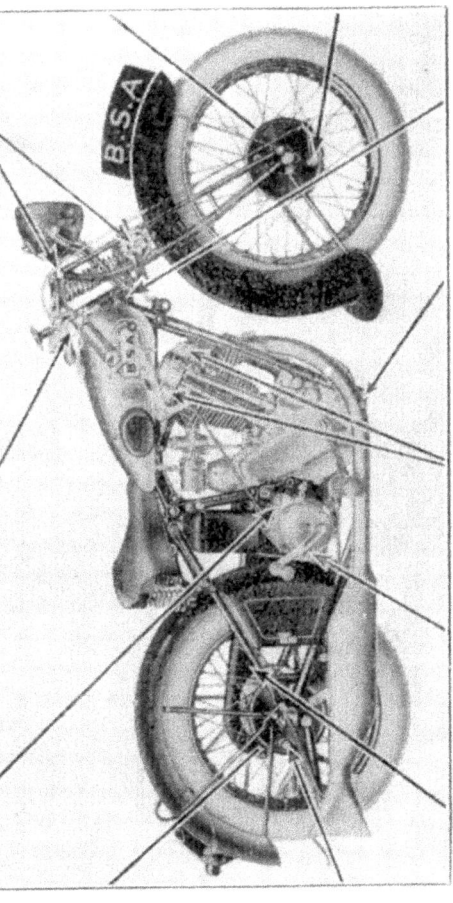

FIG. 72. LUBRICATING DIAGRAM FOR B.S.A. 3·49 H.P. O.H.V., 4·93 H.P. O.H.V., AND 4·93 H.P. O.H.V. DE LUXE MOTOR-CYCLES

the silencer (Fig. 73). It is not generally known that the noise of a motor-cycle engine is not caused by the explosion of the gas in the cylinder, but by the exhaust gas being suddenly let loose into the

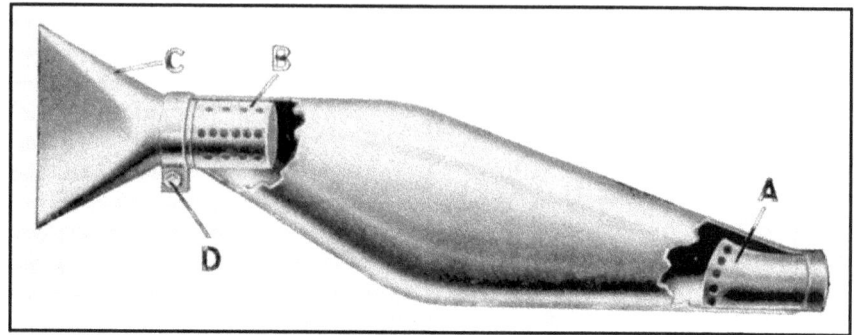

FIG. 73. THE B.S.A. SILENCER

FIG. 74.—THE CAMS FOR RAPID CHAIN ADJUSTMENT
The alignment of the wheel is automatic

air. The exhaust gases pass through the exhaust valve at a high pressure due to the explosion, and if allowed to pass from the exhaust valve directly into the air, the noise would be deafening.

Instead, it passes along the exhaust pipes into the silencer, where it expands and is expelled into the air at a lower pressure.

The silencer has a capacity of four or five times the combustion space.

It is illegal, as pointed out elsewhere, to use a cut-out, that is, a device which enables the exhaust to pass into the air without first passing through the silencer.

The silencer is of new design, and it gives a subdued and mellow note, and owing to its large capacity it offers a very small amount of back pressure to the exhaust gas, so that the power absorbed is negligible.

At the inlet side a small fish-tail A, with the sides drilled, is fixed internally in the expansion chamber. After expanding in the silencer, and thus losing both temperature and pressure, the gas passes through the drilled and blocked baffle-pipe B, and emerges into the atmosphere through the fish-tail C. The fish-tail and baffle-pipe are formed in one unit, and they may be removed from the silencer for cleaning or inspection by undoing the clip bolt D.

THE FRONT FORKS

Fig. 52, shows the type of spring fork link fitted to the B.S.A. models. These forks, it is hardly necessary to state, are for purposes of absorbing road shocks, and insulating the rider from the vibration caused. The illustrations are self-explanatory.

An important feature of B.S.A. forks is the design of the links. Long spigots formed on the links enter the fork yokes and take the entire load on the forks. A greater bearing area is thus provided, and wear on the link mechanism is considerably reduced. The space between the ends of the spigots acts as a reservoir for lubricant.

HANDLEBAR FITTING

Reversible handlebars are fitted to the 3·49 h.p. and 4·93 h.p. machines. The upturned position is suitable for touring or when the machine is used with a sidecar. When fitted downturned a sporting position is obtained.

The bars are adjustable to give a choice of wrist angle in both positions. Long rubber grips are fitted to the bars.

THE TIMING GEAR

It will have been gathered from the previous chapter that the inlet valve must remain open for about half a revolution of the crank, and the exhaust for a further half revolution. It is the purpose of the timing gear to ensure this, and a cam (see Fig. 75) lifts the inlet valve by means of an adjustable tappet, at the commencement of the suction stroke, and permits it to close at the bottom of the stroke. It operates once for every four strokes of the piston. The exhaust valve is similarly operated, commencing to open at about the end of the power stroke. The 2·49 h.p.

FIG. 75. THE B.S.A. TIMING GEAR

model has a gear-driven magneto, thus dispensing with the magneto driving chain.

BRAKES

It is law that two brakes, separately and independently operated, and each capable of stopping the machine, must be fitted. The action and specification, however, have already been given in Chapter I. The result of a recent law case makes it clear that both brakes may operate on one wheel. All B.S.A. brakes are

MECHANICAL DETAILS OF THE B.S.A.

of internal expanding hub type with large brake shoes and friction linings. They are smooth in action but extremely powerful, and retain their efficiency under all weather conditions. Means for simple and quick adjustment are provided, and the brake shoes are easily detachable for relining.

The Hinged Rear Mudguard and Rear Stand. On the 3·49 h.p. O.H.V. and larger models, the new design of rear mudguard,

FIG. 76. THE HINGED REAR MUDGUARD

which is used in conjunction with a low-lift spring-up rear stand, reduces very considerably the amount of exertion required when the rear wheel is removed for any purpose. When the machine is on the stand the rear wheel is only raised about 3 in. from the ground. It is obvious, therefore, that the effort required to raise the machine on to the stand is small. By undoing two nuts at the ends of the lower mudguard stays the hinged portion is released, and it may be swung up as shown in the illustration. The rear wheel may then be drawn clear of the machine with ease.

Hubs and Brakes. The use of taper rollers for the wheel bearings ensures that heavy loads may be carried over rough roads for prolonged periods with the minimum of wear. Adjustment is easily carried out, but owing to the substantial nature of the bearings, it is only necessary at long intervals. The large diameter high-grade steel spindle is of ample strength to withstand the most strenuous conditions. The brakes are of the internal expanding type. The brake shoes are steel pressings, light, and yet sufficiently strong to resist heavy stresses without distortion. The generous width of the linings gives a large contact area, so that a powerful retarding effect is obtained with

Fig. 77. The Hub Construction

medium brake shoe pressure. A large range of adjustment is provided for the shoes. The brake cover plate is specially formed to extend over the brake drum to render the whole weatherproof. Grease and oil from the wheel bearings are excluded from the linings by means of pen steel and felt washers. The quickly detachable front hub fitted to the 9·86 h.p. G30-16 W.T. model is slightly different in construction, but embodies all the above features.

Shock Absorbers. The advantages of properly designed shock absorbers are many. Instead of having a strong spring with a harsh rebound, the modern spring fork is fitted with a comparatively light and resilient spring, the action of which is controlled

MECHANICAL DETAILS OF THE B.S.A. 91

by the shock absorbers in such a way that the machine floats over rough surfaces without violent deflection and rapid rebound.

The B.S.A. shock absorbers consists of two steel discs A (Fig. 78) with a friction disc between them. One of the steel discs is fixed to the forks and the other to the fork link. The three discs are

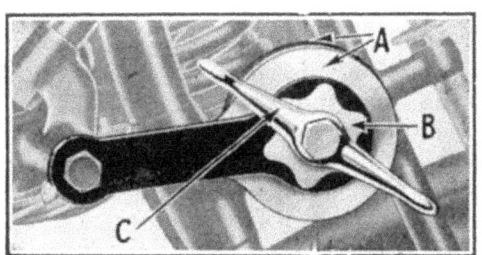

FIG. 78. THE SHOCK ABSORBERS

pressed together by means of a star spring B. When the forks deflect, the rate of movement of the links is governed by the pressure of the star spring, and this in turn is controlled by the quickly adjustable wing nut C. The quick adjustment is provided in order that the rider may alter the star spring pressure, while riding, to suit the varying road conditions encountered.

Grease Gun Lubrication. A grease-gun is supplied with the kit. To charge this, unscrew the nozzle and press the gun into position in a Tecalemit " EASY FILLING TIN " if available. Now replace the nozzle. To lubricate, place the nozzle of the gun on to the nipple, and by pushing the body of the gun down several times, grease will be forced into the working parts at high pressure. The gun can also be filled by pushing the cork piston to the far end of the gun and inserting grease into the body.

CHAPTER VI

OVERHAULING

A CAREFUL study of preceding chapters will have given the novice a fair knowledge of the construction of his machine, which, combined with the manipulative skill gained in driving, should enable him to tackle the overhaul of it.

If the engine is running well, it is best for the rider to leave it alone, except for occasionally swilling out the crankcase, as directed under the heading of riding hints.

Testing and Adjusting Tappet Clearance. The clearance between the valve tappets and the valve stems should be checked now and again, though it is unlikely that adjustment will be required unless the valves have been ground in or a new valve fitted. Always test the clearance with the engine warm, and proceed as follows—

First of all make certain that there is clearance between the bottom exhaust tappet nut and the lifting lever. This indicates that the tappet is in proper contact with the cam. It will be obvious that should the flange on the bottom tappet be resting on the lifter lever, it will prevent the tappet from forming proper contact with the cam inside the timing gear, and only partial valve lift will take place, resulting in loss of power, also speed. Turn the engine round by means of the kick-starter, with the decompressor lever down until compression is felt. Then raise the exhaust lifter and push the kick-starter down another couple of inches, so that the piston is at the top of the compression stroke or thereabouts. Now see if there is any clearance between the valve tappets and valve stems. If the clearance is correct, it should be just possible to feel a little motion when the tappet is lifted up and down with the fingers, and it should be possible to pass a piece of the paper on which this book is printed between the head of the tappet and the valve stem, but a stout visiting card should not go through. If the clearance on either valve is not correct, the tappet must be adjusted. To do this, hold the head A (Fig. 79) by means of the large end of the B.S.A. spanner, and loosen the locking sleeve B with the special tappet spanner provided (turning the handle of the spanner to the left). Then screw the head up or down to the required position, and tighten the locking sleeve again by turning the handle of the spanner to the right, meanwhile holding the

OVERHAULING 93

tappet head A with the B.S.A. spanner, and applying pressure to the left, so as to relieve from strain the small fillets which prevent the tappet rod rotating during adjustment. After tightening up, test the clearance again to make sure that it has not been altered inadvertently while tightening up. It is well worth while taking a little trouble over this tappet adjustment, as on its accuracy depends the silence of the valve gear, as well as the power obtained from the engine.

Valve Clearances on O.H.V. Machines. To ensure quiet valve-gear operation particular attention should always be paid to the clearance between valve and rocker, especially during the first 500 miles (while the working surfaces are bedding down). This should be tested when the engine is cold and with the piston at about top dead-centre at the end of the compression stroke. Test the valve clearance every 250 miles.

To check the valve clearance proceed as follows: Turn the engine round by the kick-starter until compression is felt. Then raise the exhaust lifter and push the kick-starter down another couple of inches so that the piston is at the top of the compression stroke.

There should now be clearance between the rocker and the valve stem. Owing to the pull of the rocker return springs the rocker end should be clear of the valve stem, and if pressure is exerted on the end of the rocker, movement should be felt. The clearance should be accurately checked by a set of feeler gauges. For ordinary running this should be about 3/1000-in. when the engine is cold. For racing, 4/1000-in. clearance is recommended.

If there is no clearance the valve will never close properly. Starting will be difficult and the face of the valve will become burnt and pitted due to leakage of hot gas at the moment of explosion. If the clearance is excessive the valve gear will be noisy in operation, and loss of power and increased wear will result.

In the case of the exhaust valve first make sure that the valve lifter cam inside the rocker-box is clear of the push-rod flange. It should be possible to operate the exhaust lifter lever through a small angle before moving the rocker, thus showing that the correct clearance exists. If not, the control wire should be adjusted until clearance is obtained.

TO SET THE VALVE CLEARANCE. Remove the rocker-box cover by releasing the spring clip. Undo the locking-nut A (Fig. 79) by means of the tappet spanner, and using the small end of the B.S.A. spanner turn the adjusting screw B until the correct clearance is obtained Still holding screw B tighten the locknut A. Check the clearance after tightening the locknut to make certain that this has been done correctly.

BOOK OF THE B.S.A.

Adjustment of Rockers. To adjust the overhead rockers for end-play, release locknut C (Fig. 79) and turn the adjusting nut D to the right until it just becomes tight. Then slacken it back a

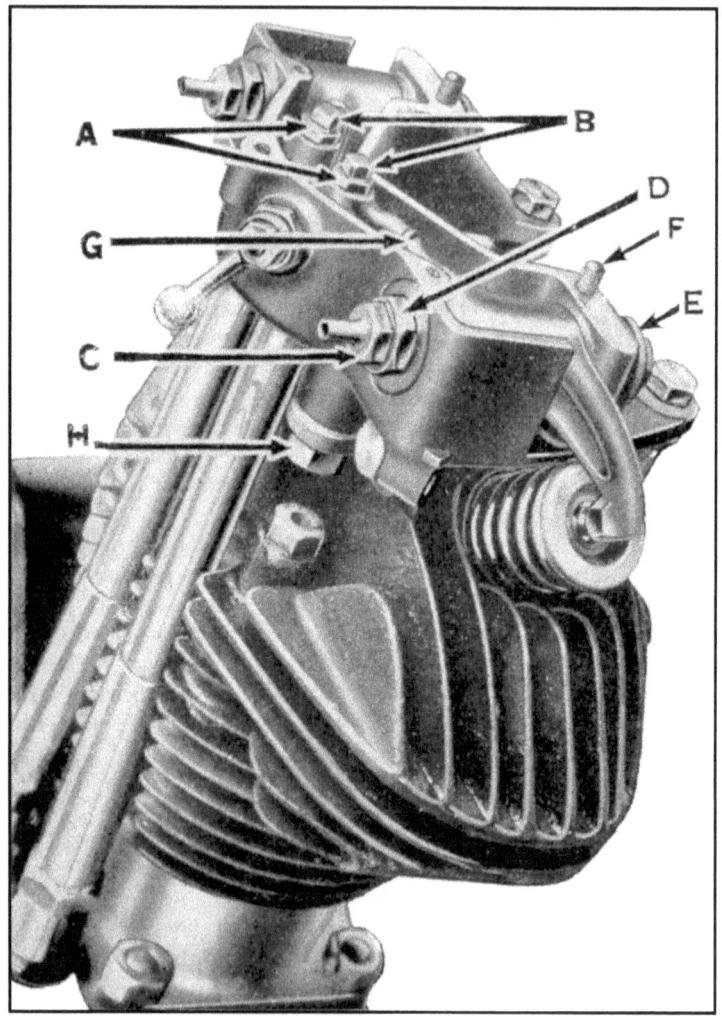

Fig. 79. Valve and Rocker Adjustments

quarter to one-third of a turn, when play should just be felt when the rocker is shaken end-ways. Then tighten the locknut.

This will be found to be the most accurate way of adjusting the rockers, since the tightening of the locknut takes up the clearance between the threads on the adjusting nut and rocker spindle.

The hexagon E should not be touched during the adjusting process. This must always be screwed up tight, and should only be unscrewed when it is desired to remove the rocker spindle. Before it can be unscrewed the locking stud F should be released by undoing the nut which is screwed on to it.

Lubrication of Rockers. Grease-gun nipples are fitted to the ends of overhead rocker spindles, and lubrication of these points should be carried out every 250 miles or weekly.

For this purpose a high melting-point graphite-impregnated grease such as Acheson's " Gredag," grade 33, is to be recommended. Speedwell " Crimsangere Heavy " may also be used.

Force the grease into the bearing by means of the grease-gun until a large amount oozes out at the ends of the rocker bearing. In this way adequate lubrication for this highly important bearing will be ensured.

Push-rod Ends. The upper push-rod ends should be lubricated once a week. To do this remove the rocker box cover and turn the engine until one of the valves is open. It will then be possible to apply oil to the push-rod end with an oil-can. This should be done for each of the push-rods in turn. Neglect to lubricate these is liable to cause wear and noise.

Oil Mist Lubrication. In addition to the system just described the valve gear is lubricated by oil mist from the engine. Oil mist formed by the splashing action of the flywheels is driven by the descending piston through holes into the timing-case, thence through grooves in the tappet guides, and up the push-rod tubes into the rocker-box. The rockers are fitted with felt rings which accumulate the oil and thus provide additional lubrication for the rocker bearings.

An important advantage of this system is that the valve and rocker gear, being enclosed, are protected from the abrasive action of dust and road grit.

The enclosing of the overhead valve gear, coupled with the efficient lubrication provided, also makes for silent operation.

Return Springs. Return springs are fitted to the push-rods (4·93 h.p. O.H.V. de luxe, 3·49 h.p. O.H.V., and 4·39 h.p. O.H.V. specially tuned engines) and to the rockers.

The push-rod return springs are held between the flange at the bottom of the push-rod and a collar at the top of the lower half of the push-rod tube (see Fig. 80). The latter is screwed on to the tappet guide, and the pressure on the spring is adjusted by screwing the tube up or down. A spring register engaging in a notch in the tube automatically locks the latter in position.

The rocker return springs are hooked on to the push-rod ends of the rockers, *G*, Fig. 79. At the other end each spring is attached to a screw having an adjusting nut, *H*. These are mounted on bosses underneath the rocker-box on each side of the push-rod tubes. To increase the tension on the rocker return spring turn the nut to the right. This operation necessitates the removal of the rocker-box. The nuts are also locked in position

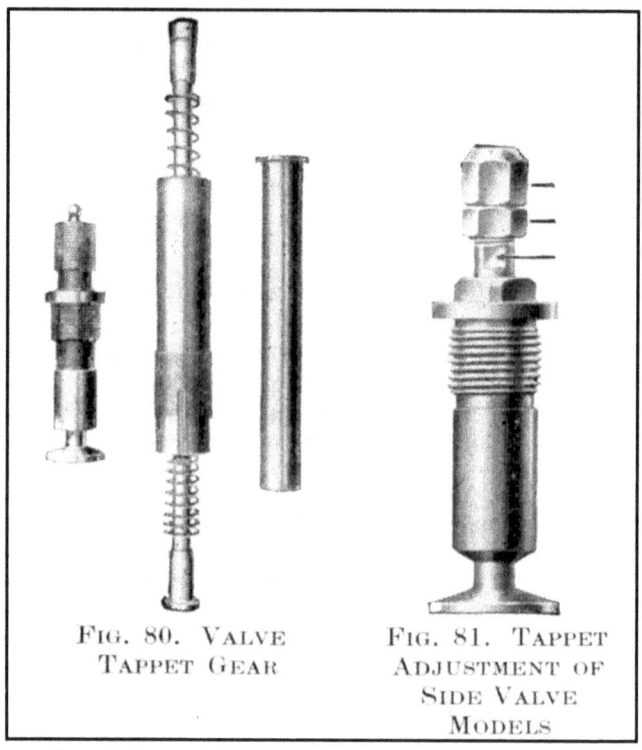

FIG. 80. VALVE TAPPET GEAR

FIG. 81. TAPPET ADJUSTMENT OF SIDE VALVE MODELS

by means of registers on their upper faces which engage in slots in the rocker return spring boss caps.

When the machine is delivered both pairs of return springs are adjusted to give medium pressure. This should not be exceeded unless maximum engine revolutions are required for racing purposes, etc. Increased loads on these springs cause greater stresses and, consequently, more rapid wear on the valve and tappet gear and cams. When high speeds are not required, or if it is desired to maintain the timing gear in an efficient condition for the longest possible period without adjustment, the pressure on the return springs should be eased right back.

Mechanical Oil Pump. If it should be necessary to remove the oil pump this should be done in the following manner: Place a tin or other receptacle under the machine to catch the oil which pours out when the pump is removed. Then unscrew the five nuts and remove the plate underneath the crankcase on the timing side. This will expose four screws which hold the pump in position. These should be removed with a screwdriver. The gauze filter will then come away and the pump can be withdrawn.

To dismantle the pump it is only necessary to remove the four screws in the cover.

When replacing the pump make certain that the driving dog on the end of the spindle engages correctly with the slot in the driving spindle.

Decarbonizing the Engine. After 1,500 miles or so have been covered, it may be necessary to decarbonize the engine. The necessity for this will be indicated by the engine becoming very liable to pink or knock, particularly when it is hot. To decarbonize it is first necessary to remove the cylinder. Proceed as follows: Detach the petrol pipe and high tension wire. Take out the sparkng plug and valve caps, and remove the compression tap. Remove the exhaust pipe, which is a push-on fit on the exhaust spigot in 2·49, 3·49 and 4·93 h.p. models, supported by a clip on the crankcase, and a push-on fit in the silencer. (In other models a screw connection is used.) Remove the carburettor by unscrewing the clip bolt on the connection between the carburettor and the cylinder. This bolt can be unscrewed by means of the small end of the B.S.A. spanner, and when it is loose the carburettor can be slid off backwards. It is as well to tie the carburettor up out of the way, preferably to the carrier stays. Now remove the four nuts which hold the cylinder to the crankcase. Lift the cylinder up and backwards into the rear angle of the frame or forwards into the front angle in the case of some of the models, and then turn the engine forwards until the piston comes out of the bottom of the cylinder, steadying the piston as it emerges, so that it shall not fall over and get cracked when it comes clear of the cylinder. Assistance may be needed for this operation. Cover the top of the crankcase with a rag to prevent grit and dust falling in.

Removing the Carbon. Remove the valves from the cylinder and carefully chip out all carbon from the top of the cylinder and the valve pocket and passages with a long-handled screwdriver. After all the carbon has been removed, swill out with paraffin and then wipe the cylinder thoroughly with a clean but oily rag. After scraping carbon off the piston, finish by polishing the top of the piston lightly with fine emery paper or metal polish, taking care not to scratch the side of the cylinder.

Examining and Removing Piston Rings. Now examine the piston rings. If they are bright and quite free in their grooves, it is better to leave them alone, as they are very brittle, and there is a considerable risk of breaking them during removal. If there are any brown patches on the rings remove them in the manner shown by Fig. 82, and fit new ones. If the rings are stuck in their grooves, prise them out very carefully and clean them.

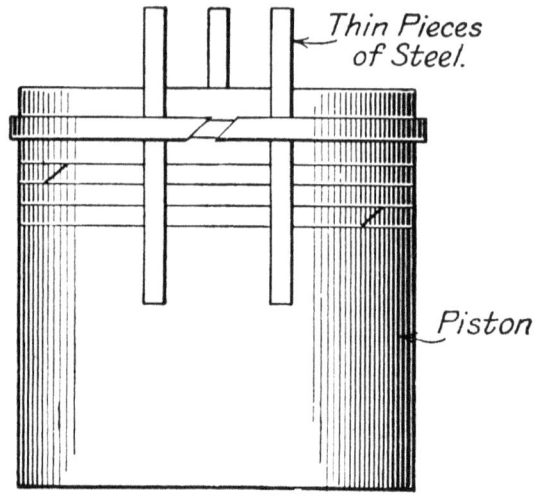

FIG. 82.—HOW TO REMOVE PISTON RINGS

after soaking in paraffin to soften the carbon. Scrape any carbon from the grooves and from the inside and edges of the rings, and then replace, providing they are otherwise in order. If, however, the machine is used for speed work, the lower piston ring may be discarded with advantage.

Position of Piston Ring Gaps. After cleaning the piston, make sure that the slots in the piston rings are on the opposite sides of the piston to one another, and then smear the sides of the piston generously with engine oil, to obviate any risk of damage when first running after assembly.

Cleaning Out the Crankcase. While the cylinder is off, it is advisable to clean out the crankcase. This is done by unscrewing the drain plug on the bottom right-hand side of the crankcase and allowing the oil to drain out. The crankcase should then be swilled out with paraffin and the plug replaced. Make sure that the latter is screwed up tight.

Reassembling the Engine. After this has been done, the engine may be reassembled. Hold the cylinder in the rear angle of the frame and place the piston a little before bottom dead centre on the downward stroke. The cylinder should then slide home quite easily. Replace the cylinder nuts, making sure they are tight, and then fit the valve caps and compression tap. The carburettor petrol pipe, high tension wire, and exhaust pipe may then be replaced.

Running the Engine after Assembly. Before starting up the engine open the valve fully on the oil sight drip feed on the oil tank, and give at least three complete charges of lubricating oil to the engine. This is very important and must be kept in mind. After this has been done, adjust the oil valve to give its usual supply of oil, according to whether the machine is used for sidecar or solo work respectively.

The engine should then be ready for the road again, but full power cannot be expected until it has had a little running in to allow valves and piston rings to become properly bedded in.

Valve Timing. The valve timing of the engine should not be tampered with in any way, as the makers' setting is that which has been found to give the best results. Should the timing be disturbed, however, the engine should be revolved until the tooth on the small pinion, with a dash mark on it, is at the top. The inlet cam pinion should then be inserted in such a way that the space, also marked with a dash, is occupied by the marked tooth on the small pinion. The space on exhaust cam pinion marked with a dot should then be engaged with the tooth also marked with a dot on the inlet pinion.

How to Grind-in the Valves. If either of the valves is slightly pitted on its seat it may be ground in by smearing the coned faces with a coarse emery paste, replacing the valve on its seat, and rotating the valve on it by means of a screwdriver placed in the slot in the crown of the valve. This will rapidly effect the removal of uneven places, and when an even surface shows the faces should be wiped clean and a thin even paste of flour emery applied. Rotate the valve as before by means of the screwdriver until a dead smooth surface results. If it is badly pitted, however, it should be sent to the B.S.A. works at Birmingham to be refaced. On its return a very slight amount of grinding-in will be sufficient to make a good face. Never attempt to grind in a badly pitted valve, as excessive valve grinding wears away the valve seat in the cylinder and causes the valve to become pocketed with consequent loss of power. (See Fig. 83.) After grinding-in, be very careful to wipe away all traces of the grinding material, both on the valve and in the cylinder.

Magneto Timing. To re-time the magneto, first loosen the chain sprocket, remove the contact breaker cover and compression tap. Rotate the engine in a forward direction until the inlet valve closes. Now insert a rod or wire through the compression tap hole, and move the engine still farther, until the piston is felt to be at the top of its stroke. Move the contact breaker by means of the control lever or twist grip on the handlebar until it is fully retarded, and then turn the magneto shaft until the platinum points are just about to break. Lightly tighten the magneto sprocket, and then check the timing by again finding

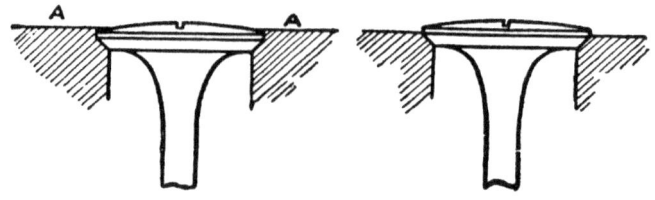

FIG. 83.—DIAGRAM SHOWING HOW VALVES BECOME POCKETED AFTER FREQUENT REGRINDING

the top of the compression stroke and examining the position of points. If correct, finally tighten up sprocket nut.

Adjusting the Magneto Chain. To adjust the magneto chain, slacken the two bolts at side of magneto platform and remove chain cover plate. Now slide magneto backward or forward to required position and tighten up bolts. Afterwards test the chain tension. This should be such that the slightest possible amount of up and down movement can be felt in centre of chain. If the chain is too tight, a grinding noise will be noticeable, while too slack a chain will cause a rattling noise.

Adjusting the Magneto. This requires no lubrication whatever. Test the clearance between the contact points P (Fig. 84) by means of the gauge attached to magneto spanner. If incorrect, adjust the point, first releasing the lock-nut at end of pin opposite to contact. Occasionally clean the points by brushing over with petrol applied with a small brush.

Sparking Plug. Clean the sparking plug points occasionally and adjust the gap to between $\frac{1}{64}$ in. and $\frac{1}{32}$ in. Make the gap as large as possible, however, consistent with easy starting, as a wide spark gap means a hot spark, which, in turn, ensures satisfactory running, and lessens the tendency for the points to become sooted up.

Care of Chains. It is advisable to remove both chains periodically. Remove chains by detaching the spring link. They should then be thoroughly cleansed in petrol or paraffin and dried off. Immerse them for some time at about the temperature of boiling water in a mixture of grease and graphite. After they have cooled wipe off the excess lubricant. Under load the lubricant will be gradually squeezed out; the process should therefore be

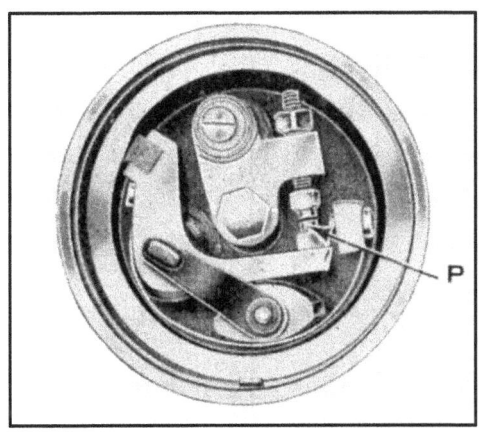

FIG. 84.—THE MAKE-AND-BREAK PORTION OF THE MAGNETO ; P = CONTACT POINTS

repeated, say, every 1,000 miles. Clean the sprockets and, on replacing the chain, note that the split end of the spring fastener is at the rear to direction of travel of chain.

Adjusting the Front Driving Chain. For front chain adjustment the gear-box is made to swivel on its lower anchoring bolt while the top bolt slides in specially-shaped slots in the cradle plates. The screw adjuster for moving the gear-box is mounted on the right-hand at the front (Fig. 86).

To adjust the chain slacken off nuts L and release lock-nut M. To tighten the chain turn hexagon head N to the left; to make the chain slack turn to the right.

The chain when properly adjusted should have about $\frac{5}{8}$ in. freedom up or down at the centre at the tightest portion of the drive.

Make sure that the nuts L are well tightened after moving the gear-box. If a considerable movement has been made in the position of gear-box, it will be necessary to re-adjust the gear control rod. To effect this, the lever B should be moved towards the front of the machine until the spring plunger inside gear-box can be felt to have registered with its recess (lever will now be approximately in the upright position). The nuts C should now be slackened from sleeve D, bearing in mind that the lower one

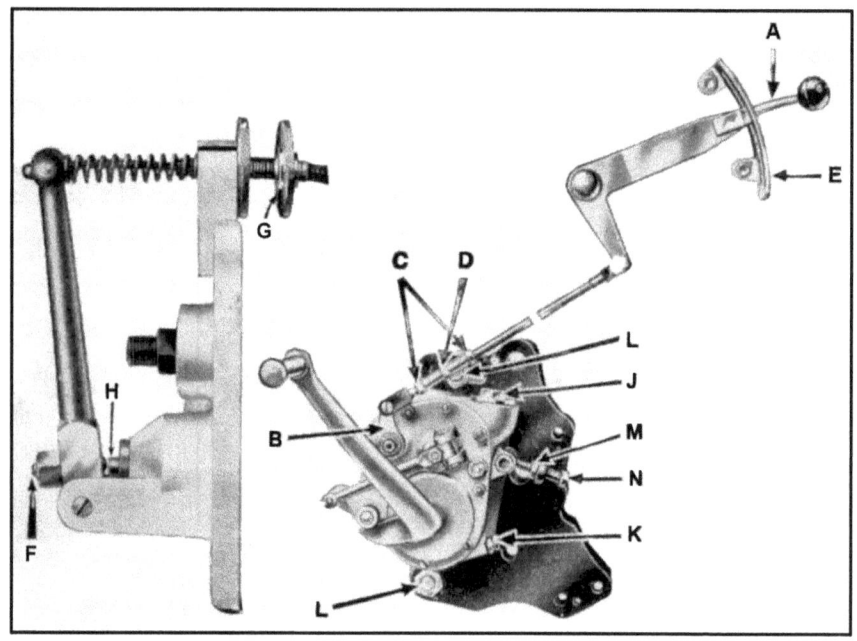

FIGS. 85 AND 86.—HOW TO ADJUST THE FRONT CHAIN

has a left-hand thread. Sleeve D should now be moved until operating lever A is just making contact with the end of its quadrant, as at E. Then tighten nuts C. Test adjustment by moving lever to middle of neutral position, noting that the spring plunger can be felt engaging when the lever A is opposite the respective position on the quadrant. The clutch can be adjusted by means of either screw F or G, the lock-nuts having first been released. The screws should then be adjusted until a slight clearance is perceptible between screw F and rod H.

Adjusting the Rear Chain. To adjust the rear chain, loosen the nut on the hub spindle on the left side of the machine; then the nut on the right side. Apply an adjustable spanner (handle upwards) to the square end of the hub spindle, then turn towards the front of the machine until the chain is tight. Slightly turn the reverse way to slacken the chain sufficiently to ensure free running. Hold the spanner firmly in this position, keeping the cams and blocks in close contact, then with the other spanner tighten the left-hand nut, remove the adjustable spanner and tighten up the right-hand spindle nut. This chain should have a sag of about $\frac{1}{2}$ in. when properly adjusted. It may be found necessary to adjust the rear brake after adjusting the rear chain.

Hub Adjustment. Both front and rear hubs (shown in section in Figs. 87 and 88 respectively) are of the taper roller bearing type. They should be tested frequently for side-play and adjusted if necessary. To adjust for side-play slacken off the left-hand spindle nut A and turn the bearing nut B gradually, at the same time rotating the wheel slowly and testing for side-play. When the play is all taken up unscrew the nut B about one-third of a turn or until play can just be felt when the wheel is rocked sideways. Upon tightening up the spindle nut A this play will be taken up, and the adjustment will be correct if there is the barest perceptible shake in the bearing as measured at the wheel rim.

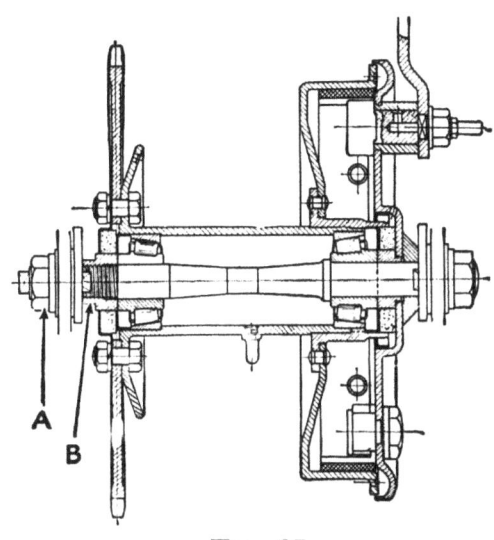

FIG. 87

Do not screw the bearing nut B up too tight when making the preliminary adjustment or the rollers and races may be damaged.

It is essential that the wheel bearings should be free but without excessive play, and this adjustment should be very carefully made and checked.

On the 1·74 h.p. model slacken off the left-hand spindle nut A and turn the left-hand cone B (Fig. 89) with the flat cone spanner supplied in the tool kit until the cone becomes tight. Then unscrew the cone about one-third of a turn or until play in the bearing can just be felt when the wheel is rocked sideways. Upon tightening up the spindle nut A this play will be taken up, and the adjustment will be correct if there is the barest susceptible shake in the bearing as measured at the wheel rim.

It is essential that the bearing should be free, but without excessive play, and this adjustment should be very carefully made and checked.

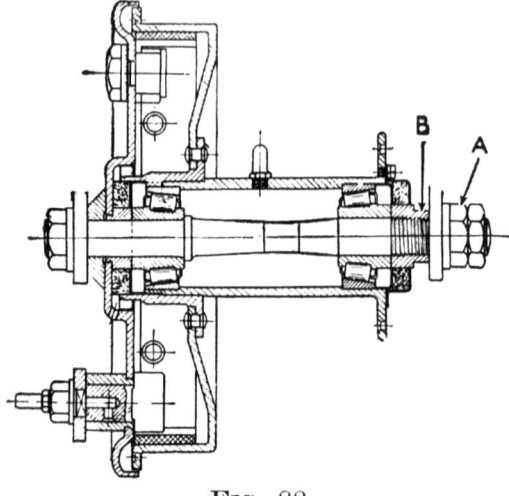

FIG. 88

Brake Adjustment. Quick adjustment is provided for the brakes. To adjust the rear brake it is only necessary to screw the wing-nut fixed to the end of the brake rod backwards or forwards, as the case may be, until the correct setting is obtained.

To adjust the front brake the sleeve mounted on the front fork yoke lug should be screwed in or out. The end of the Bowden cable outer casing fits into this sleeve. The sleeve lock-nut should be released before adjustment and tightened afterwards.

Hub and Brake Lubrication. It is of the utmost importance that the hubs should be greased every 250 miles, or weekly. If this is not done they are liable to overheat and wear. Care should be taken, however, to avoid over-lubricating the hubs, since any

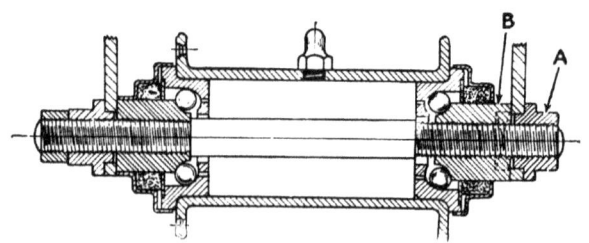

FIG. 89. DIAGRAM SHOWING HOW TO ADJUST THE HUB BEARINGS ON THE 1·74 H.P. TWO-STROKE MODEL

excess of grease may reach the brake linings and impair the efficiency of the brakes. When the machines are sent out the hubs are packed with grease, and the regular weekly application of a small quantity will maintain this amount.

The brake cams should be greased every 1,000 miles, or monthly.

OVERHAULING

Only a small quantity of grease should be applied, otherwise the linings may be affected.

Dismantling the Clutch. To dismantle the clutch the nut Y must be removed. The end-plate R and spring X will now slide

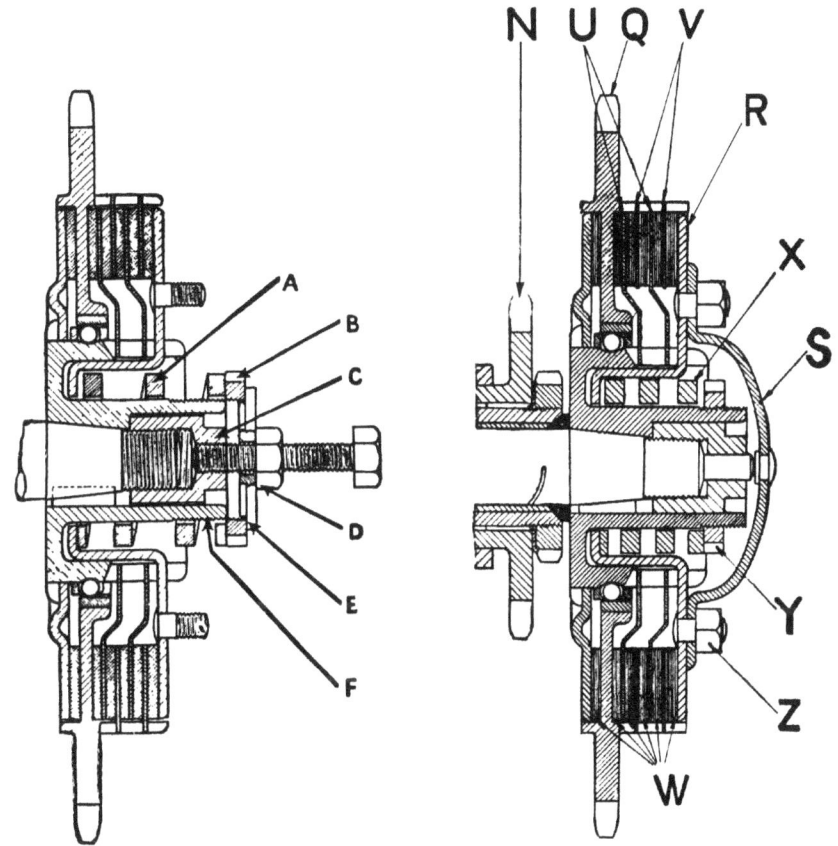

FIGS. 90 AND 91.—CROSS-SECTION OF THE B.S.A. CLUTCH

Showing bolt, nut, and large washer used for dismantling and assembling the clutch

off, leaving the plates accessible. Note the order in which the plates U, V, and W are arranged, so that they can be assembled in the same order (see Figs. 90 and 91). Thoroughly cleanse by means of a stiff brush and petrol, removing all trace of oil or grease, and when dry reassemble.

In assembling the clutch the pressure of the spring A (Fig. 90) has to be overcome before the nut B can be engaged on its thread.

To enable this to be done a thread has been formed in the nut C, into which the set-screw supplied in the kit may be engaged when the clutch-operating rod has been removed.

It will be seen that by means of the nut D and washer E the nut B may be forced up to the threaded portion F against the pressure of the spring A. When in this position, if the nuts B and D are turned together the former nut will engage on its thread.

Refit cap and make sure that the nuts Z are tight. Instructions for adjusting clutch, control, etc., will be found on the countershaft three-speed and free-engine gear control.

The clutch cable should be greased periodically. This calls for its withdrawal from the outer casing, and the cable should be examined at the ends. If any of the wires are frayed, difficulty will be experienced in re-inserting the cable, and a new one should be fitted.

Cleaning the Machine. The life of the machine is increased and its appearance and value greatly improved by regular and careful attention to cleaning. Especial care should be taken near all moving parts, so as to prevent grit working in and causing undue wear and other troubles. Particularly is this the case round the front, rear, and sidecar hubs, carburettor, magneto, valve stems, tappets, front brake and gear-box. Never remove dry and caked mud from the frame, mudguards, etc. To do so means that the enamel will be subjected to the abrasive action of the grit, and the polish will soon be destroyed. Thoroughly soak the dirt first, then wash it off and wipe the parts dry. If a hosepipe is available, this will be found the most satisfactory way of removing dirt. Direct the stream of water on the portion being cleaned, taking care to avoid playing direct on to the hub bearings, etc. Afterwards brush lightly with a soft brush, finally drying and polishing with chamois leather. To remove dirt from the engine, soak it well with paraffin and cleanse with a fresh supply, then wipe dry. To remove oil stains from the crankcase use caustic soda solution. An occasional coating of a cylinder paint should be given to prevent rusting of the cylinder, or a solution of lamp black in paraffin to which a small quantity of gold size has been added may be used. This will also be found to assist the radiation of heat.

The Front Forks. Lubricate the front fork link bearings frequently.

Keep the link bolts tight enough to eliminate side-play, which generally causes a mechanical click. To adjust, unscrew the nuts on the left-hand side and screw up the bolts from the right-hand side just sufficiently tight to eliminate all side play, then lock in position with the nuts, doing one bolt at a time. If too tight, the flexibility of the fork will be reduced.

To Remove the Front Fork Spring. Support the crankcase on a box, so that the front wheel stands clear of the ground. Remove the nut from top spring retaining bolt, and depress same until it can be removed from anchorage lug, afterwards " unwinding " spring from bottom retaining scroll. Then remove the four bolts from the forks by unscrewing the nuts on the left-hand side and withdrawing from the right. Slide out the four links sideways and the forks will fall clear of the machine, and the spring may be lifted off.

The Steering Head. Frequent attention should also be paid to the steering head. A lubricator is fitted on the right-hand side at the bottom of ball head, and thin oil should preferably be used. If this point is not oiled regularly the head will become stiff and the steering will feel unsteady. Therefore oil regularly. To adjust head, unscrew the clip nut, screw down the adjusting nut by means of a special spanner supplied with tool kit until there is no perceptible shake in head, slack back about a twelfth of a turn, and then screw up clip nut again tightly.

Lubricating the Gears. The efficiency and life of the gears will be greatly increased if the following instructions are carefully adhered to. Remove the oil plugs, already referred to, on end plate of gear-box to drain the old oil out, and inject the proper grade of cylinder or gear-box oil until the oil level rises to the top of filler hole when machine is in upright position. This level should be maintained by frequent injections. After every 1,500 miles running, thoroughly flush with paraffin. To do this the machine should be started on the stand, top gear afterwards being engaged with clutch in. Remove the gear-box cover and pour in clean paraffin. With the engine running the gears will be swilled clean, and the paraffin should be drained out by means of the drain plug. Carefully drain by means of the plug provided, afterwards refilling with oil to the correct level. Care should be taken that the clearance between screw F and rod H is maintained (see instructions for adjusting), otherwise the full spring pressure will not be operating on the plates, and clutch will be continually slipping.

Pipe Joints. It is essential that the whole of the joints of the pipes, etc., made between the tank, sight feed, and engine, should be quite airtight, and in the event of a collection of oil in the sight feed which fails to clear itself, the non-return washer, situated under the sight feed, should be inspected. This non-return washer consists of a small pen-steel disc working in a brass socket and prevents blow back from the engine. It will be necessary in this case to ascertain that this has not become displaced, or has been prevented from properly seating itself through dirty or congealed oil. The parts in question should be cleaned and the final delivery pipe should also be inspected for a partial stoppage when this trouble will, without doubt, be overcome.

Alignment of the B.S.A. Sidecar. The 4·93 h.p. and higher powered models only are designed for a sidecar, connections being formed integral with the frame.

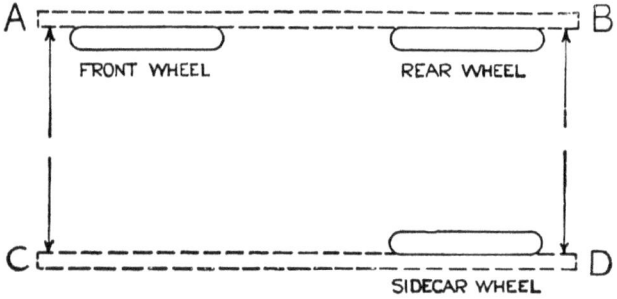

FIG. 92.—HOW TO ALIGN THE SIDECAR

It is essential for the life of the machine that the sidecar is correctly aligned, and Fig. 92 shows how this should be carried out. Lay a long wooden straight edge (*A*–*B*) along both wheels of the motor-bicycle, and a similar straight edge (*C*–*D*) along the sidecar wheel. Make certain that the machine is perfectly upright ; then adjust the sidecar until the points *A* and *C* are $\frac{1}{2}$ in. closer together than the points *B* and *D*.

For the purpose of alignment, the main sidecar connection is provided with adjusting washers, two of which are at the chassis end of the main front arm and four on the footboard connection. These are supplied loose and are to be used in lining up the machine, if necessary, to obtain the correct alignment as in the diagram above.

The rear connection is fitted with spherical washer and spring washer to facilitate the vertical alignment of the machine. Lock up tightly after the correct alignment has been obtained. It is important that any vertical alignment should be released at the bolts on the twin tubes of the chassis.

Care should be taken to refit all castellated nuts with split cotter pins.

Coiling Petrol Pipes. Figs. 93 and 94 show the correct and incorrect methods of forming the coils in petrol pipes. It will be noticed that an air lock (a common trouble) is caused when the

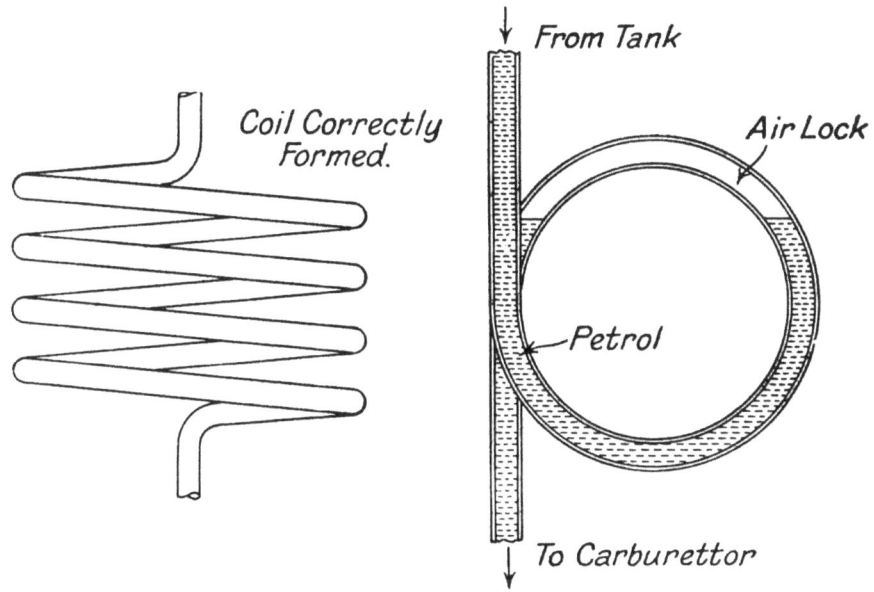

FIGS. 93 AND 94.—THE CORRECT AND INCORRECT METHODS OF COILING PETROL PIPES

coils are formed with a horizontal axis. They should, of course, have a vertical axis.

Removing Tight Studs. Fig. 95 shows the method of removing studs for purposes of replacement. Two nuts are locked together, and a spanner used on the *bottom* one to unscrew the stud.

Paper Washers. These are useful in preventing leakage, and may be made by placing a sheet of paper over the part for which the washer is intended and rubbing round the edge. A clear impression is thus made on the paper.

Truing Wheels. The preliminary operation is first to ascertain the extent of warp or deviation from the circular, and this is done by spinning the rim between the forks, holding a piece of chalk to the rim, so that the hit-and-miss places are clearly marked. Where the rim rises and falls, the spokes at those parts must be respectively tightened or slackened. If the wheel is " out of flat " (lack of truth sideways) the spokes must be tightened on one side and loosened on the other. It is a fiddling operation requiring great care. A nipple key should be used for turning the nipples.

Having trued the wheels sideways and circumferentially, pass a cord through the spokes and stretch it taut so that it lies diagonally across the oil-hole of the hub, so that it touches the rim

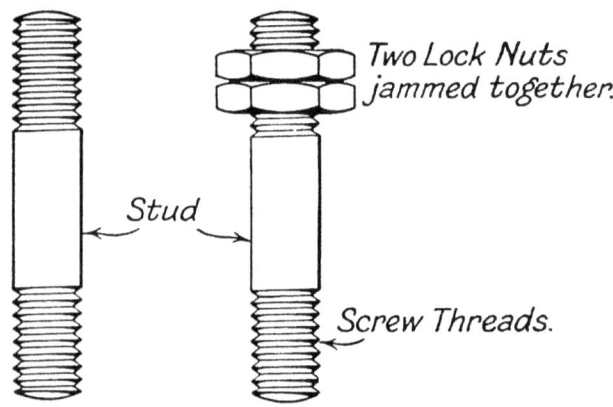

FIG. 95.—HOW TO REMOVE STUDS

on opposing sides. Next reverse the position of the diagonal, so that it touches the other two opposing sides. If the wheel is not pulled over on the hub, the string should pass through the centre of the oil-hole in both instances.

The spokes when plucked with the fingers should all yield the same note. If at any time it is necessary to remove the rim from the spokes, perhaps to change rims or remove a dent, and the rider is uncertain about wheel building, before removing the nipples obtain some fine copper wire and tie the spokes together at the point where they intercept one another. Then remove the nipples and carefully spring the spokes out of place, which will leave them in their proper position on the hub.

Re-enamelling. With so many excellent enamels on the market, the amateur can obtain excellent results if at the time of overhauling he considers the frame needs enamelling. If time and expense warrant it, he is, however, advised to have it stoved, a special process of *baking* the enamel on, which cannot be done at home without special plant. The frame should be stripped of fittings and scraped down to the bare metal with an old knife, or the edge of a piece of glass, and then polished absolutely bright and smooth with emery cloth. This is important, for any imperfections in the surface, such as roughness or rust, will affect the finished surface. The modern cellulose finishes are also recommended.

Then give a coat of enamel of the desired colour. When this is thoroughly dry, dull its surface with very fine glasspaper, and apply a second coat. Repeat this process until four or five coats have been applied, when a coat of varnish should be evenly brushed on and left to get thoroughly hard.

The work should be carried out in a warm room or shed, and when applying the varnish, the floor should be sprinkled with water to lay the dust.

The varnish should be left to dry, keeping doors and windows shut to exclude all dust, which, if allowed to enter, will settle on the varnish, causing the latter to dry with a gritty surface.

Lining transfers are on the market, and if used should be applied before the coat of varnish.

CHAPTER VII

TOURING

MOTOR-cycle touring to-day is almost as certain as travelling by railway, and is, if anything, less costly and certainly much healthier. There is the added pleasure of being able to vary one's rate of progress at will—lingering amongst pleasant scenery and hurrying through the drab portions. The important questions are those of dress, luggage, tools, equipment, maps and guides.

DRESS

Personal comfort is of first importance, and all the delights of the weather and the countryside are liable to be lost sight of if it is not attained. It is wise to remember the humour and even contempt with which a certain type of motor-cyclist is regarded. You know the sort—the owner of one of the lightest of light-weights who will dash round the country at the alarming rate of about 12 miles an hour, clad in a heavy leather suit, goggles, heavy crash helmet and Wellingtons. Do not follow his example. Select your dress with due regard to utility, comfort and appearance. There is little need to provide special clothing for pottering. Protection from dust is all that is needed, and a light coat of the dustproof variety fills the bill. Apart from penetrating one's clothing, dust can also produce painful results if a sharp piece gets under the eyelids, and for this reason goggles are an essential part of the equipment. One's ordinary clothes may be used, but there is always the risk of splashing them with oil, or otherwise spoiling them. It is cheaper in the long run, if a great deal of riding is to be done, to have a special dress consisting of riding breeches and leggings or stockings, the dustproof coat (of the sports coat type), and goggles.

Goggles. A word or so here about goggles is advisable. Goggles are obtainable in a variety of forms, from the one-piece celluloid pattern to the spectacle type having two oval lenses, which may be replaced when broken. The former, the writer finds, are extremely comfortable to wear, and as well the field of vision is not so restricted as with the lens type. Goggles with tinted glasses are also available, and in bright sunlight are extremely restful to the eyes. One has only to ride with the sun glaring in one's eyes for any distance to realize what " sun-blindness " is, and the feeling of helplessness which accompanies it.

These coloured glasses (blue and yellow are useful colours) lessen the possibility of this.

Another type of goggles which has the laudable object of saving the eyes of the rider in the event of accident is the Triplex goggles. Each lens of this consists of two layers of glass with a layer of celluloid between, and although in the case of an accident they may crack, they do not actually break.

There is another point connected with goggles which receives all too little attention. It is the *fit* of them. Goggles which do not fit closely to the face will cause colds in the eyes and eye soreness, and even dust may enter the eye. See to it, then, that the goggles fit close to the face.

All Weather Riding. Whilst it cannot be gainsaid that spring and summer riding is pleasanter, autumn and winter riding, providing the day is not wet, is not without its charm.

Winter clothing is certainly on a more elaborate scale than summer clothing. Underclothing, which in summer is of the light " summer-weight " variety, should be of the heavy woollen winter quality. The commonest type of winter dress, and one which withal is the cheapest, consists of the ordinary buff waterproof coat and leggings, the latter lacing or buttoning up the sides. They may be purchased from most accessory dealers. An objection to them is that they soon show grease marks, and even when fitting nicely lack that smart appearance which the average motor cyclist requires. Another objection is the awkward operation of lacing or buttoning the leggings, especially if the fingers are cold.

A much more satisfactory " all weather " apparel consists of a brown oilskin coat, of such a length that it barely covers the knees. To have it longer is to make kick-starting awkward, and to run the risk of portions getting caught in the transmission or spokes. Two patterns are made—one which buttons together and one which straps together. The writer prefers the latter, as it is possible to pull it more closely to the body, under which condition it is warmer and excludes penetrating draughts.

The apparel for the legs to be worn with the oilskin for winter riding may consist of that already recommended, but undoubtedly the best form of mud and water excluder is a pair of waders, which somewhat resemble fishermen's waders. They may appear ungainly, but they do keep one dry, and enable one to arrive at the destination clean and dry underneath, and there is no risk of the trousers becoming soiled.

Overall suits of light material enable one's ordinary attire to be worn underneath, and upon arriving at the home of, say, one's sweetheart, it is merely necessary to remove the overalls to present a spick and span appearance. If anything, they are more suited to summer riding, but plenty of riders wear them all the year round.

Headwear. It has already been stated that a cap is most satisfactory, and it should be of such a fit that it may be worn peak to the front, with little risk of being blown off. Some riders wear caps peak to the back, for one of two reasons. Either the cap is too large and blows off when correctly worn, or they wish in their vanity to be regarded as racing motor cyclists. The peak helps to keep the sun from the eyes, and its only objection is that it is in the way when raising the goggles.

A felt hat of the soft, or trilby, pattern is comfortable if of good fit, and is cooler to wear in summer than a cap.

The helmet undoubtedly is advisable for those who intend to ride long distances in all weathers, for while it must be admitted that some wear them to "look the part," it is entirely wrong to assume that only racing men should wear them. They are preferred because they are extremely comfortable in use, eliminate the whistle of the wind past one's ears when travelling in a wind or at fairly high speed, are quite weatherproof, and do not blow off. Helmets of the crash type are intended for competition work, and for such are advised. Those likely to have much riding to do in wet weather may find the fisherman's "sou'-wester," perhaps, even more serviceable than a helmet.

Several other garments are marketed. Woollen cardigans having long sleeves, and intended to be worn in conjunction with sleeved leather waistcoats are intended as aids to warmth. In all cases avoid the loud extreme, if you do not wish to be a standing joke among your friends.

Gloves. The problem of keeping the hands warm and at the same time enabling them to finger the controls sensitively, is a difficult one. Ordinary fleece-lined gloves allow the air to blow up the sleeve. To obviate this, gauntlets may be worn. These have an extension which fits over the coat sleeve. The difficulty with gloves and gauntlets, however, is that the fingers "fumble" the controls, and are not nearly so sensitive.

The writer does not recommend woollen gloves, for they are liable to become caught in the controls and, say, drag the throttle lever open at the very moment when it is desired to be closed.

An attempt to solve the glove difficulty has been made by one or two firms who market a rubber muff, like the extension of the gauntlet glove. This fits over and beyond the grips of the handlebars, so that the hands are sheltered and the wind deflected.

Leg Shields. The obvious object of these is to keep the clothing clean and dry, and in muddy weather they undoubtedly do keep a considerable amount off, but the very wide and efficient mudguarding of the B.S.A. machine renders their use almost unnecessary. They usually screw on to the footboards and clip on to the frame.

Windscreens. Lately windscreens have been marketed which attach to the handlebars and prevent the face from getting cold.

LUGGAGE

The question of what luggage to carry on a tour depends to a great extent on the length of the tour and the type of machine. The point of view to adopt is : What can I do without ? Not : What can I do with ?

For a week-end tour one obviously must take night attire, a clean shirt and vest, two clean collars (to provide a margin for accidents with greasy fingers), shaving tackle, tooth brush, brush and comb, soft hat or cap, and socks. With regard to clothing, although space may be found for it, it is well to travel in the suit one desires to wear, and to protect it in the manner already noted under " Dress." It must be remembered that on a solo machine only a small suit case can be accommodated, as only the carrier is available for it, but with a sidecar, even though a passenger be carried, there is the additional space afforded by the locker, and small items can easily be accommodated in with the passenger. All bags should be packed as tightly as possible to avoid damage by road vibration.

If the tour is to last for a week or a fortnight, carry only sufficient clothing for immediate needs, and arrange for underclothing, etc., to be sent on to an appropriate destination, returning the soiled apparel by the same means.

INCIDENTAL MATTERS

Spares. There is little need to carry more than a repair outfit, pump, usual tools, as supplied with the machine, spare plugs, spare tubes, spare chains (or chain and belt) and chain extractor or belt punch, and spare valves and valve springs.

Useful oddments such as cones, bolts, nuts, chain-coupling links, insulating tape, electric bulbs and/or burners can be packed in a small box with pieces of rag stuffed between to prevent rattle and damage

Maps and Guides. These are quite a necessary adjunct to touring, and, indeed, the fascination of planning a tour is part of its pleasure. The route should be traced out in red ink on the map, and the sidecar passenger is then able to direct the driver by following the map in conjunction with the direction taken. A contour road book is useful, in that it enables one to pick the flattest route. Ordnance survey maps are recommended, or Bartholomew's, and a scale of one mile or two miles to the inch is preferred. So complete and comprehensive are these maps that finding one's way is simplicity itself. It should here be mentioned that Messrs. Michelin publish an excellent road guide almost indispensable to the tourist, for in it is a list of the hotels and repairers for every village and town in the United Kingdom. Additionally, the distance from one town to another is given, and street plans of important towns are presented. It is a wonderful compilation, deservedly popular and quite interesting to read. The Dunlop Tyre Company issue a work of equal merit, and either of the volumes can be recommended.

The Tour in Prospect. If the reader is considering a tour and is a member of one of the Associations mentioned in Chapter II, it is well to remember that these offer special touring facilities to their members, and accordingly the secretary should be apprised of the intended route. Especially is this necessary when a continental tour is to be undertaken, for the Society sees to the obtaining of the members' passports, carnets or triptiques, and renders unnecessary the leaving of deposits when going into a foreign land to satisfy legal requirements regarding the law of imports and exports.

Taking the Machine Abroad. The triptique referred to in the last paragraph enables the owner to travel in Finland, Holland, France, Italy, Switzerland, Belgium, Portugal, Spain, Rumania, Russia, Norway and Sweden, or as an alternative he can be equipped with an International Customs Pass, issued by the A.C.U. and A.A. to members and non-members, whereby the highest continental duty payable suffices for all the countries forming part of the Convention.

International Travelling Passes (lasting 12 months) are also issued, enabling the holders to travel in all countries which are parties to the agreement, without obtaining special licences or carrying special numbers in each country as hitherto. The Customs Pass concerns the customs duty payable ; the Travelling Pass is exclusively a licence for the machine and driver abroad.

Up-to-date information about the best means of transit and the best routes is also supplied, and may save a lot of trouble.

It is not nowadays required of the tourist to submit to being examined by a foreign official, to obtain foreign licences,

TOURING

temporary foreign number, or any other of the onerous formalities
It is only necessary to obtain the International pass, and fix an
oval plate to the machine with the letters G.B. painted in white
on a black ground. This plate must be illuminated at night.

Continental Rule of the Road, etc. As a general rule *Keep to
the Left* and *Pass on the Right* in Austria, Hungary, Portugal
and Sweden.

As a general rule *Keep to the Right* and *Pass on the Left* in
Belgium, France, Germany, Holland, Italy, Russia, Spain,
Switzerland, and also in Carinthia (Austria), Carniola, Dalmatia,
Istria, and Tyrol.

The speed limit in Belgium is 40 kilom. an hour in the country,
and 15 in town. Special regulations apply to Brussels. Motor-
cycles may use the paths made specially for cyclists. The
Belgian roads (except in some districts) are exceedingly bad.

Lamps must be lit in France not later than fifteen minutes

LIGHTING-UP TIME TABLE
(Greenwich Mean Time)

Add One Hour during Summer Time Period

	JANUARY				JULY		
1	4.30 p.m.	22	5. 1 p.m.	2	8.48 p.m.	23	8.29 p.m.
8	4.39 ,,	29	5.12 ,,	9	8.45 ,,	30	8.20 ,,
15	4.49 ,,			16	8.38 ,,		
	FEBRUARY				AUGUST		
5	5.25 p.m.	19	5.51 p.m.	6	8. 8 p.m.	20	7.41 p.m.
12	5.38 ,,	26	6. 3 ,,	13	7.55 ,,	27	7.27 ,,
	MARCH				SEPTEMBER		
5	6.14 p.m.	19	6.40 p.m.	3	7.11 p.m.	17	6.39 p.m.
12	6.28 ,,	26	6.51 ,,	10	6.56 ,,	24	6.23 ,,
	APRIL				OCTOBER		
2	7. 3 p.m.	23	7.38 p.m.	1	6. 7 p.m.	22	5.20 p.m.
9	7.14 ,,	30	7.49 ,,	8	5.51 ,,	29	5. 8 ,,
16	7.26 ,,			15	5.35 ,,		
	MAY				NOVEMBER		
7	8. 1 p.m.	21	8.20 p.m.	5	4.55 p.m.	19	4.34 p.m.
14	8.11 ,,	28	8.30 ,,	12	4.43 ,,	26	4.27 ,,
	JUNE				DECEMBER		
4	8.38 p.m.	18	8.48 p.m.	3	4.22 p.m.	24	4.23 p.m.
11	8.44 ,,	25	8.49 ,,	10	4.19 ,,	31	4.19 ,,
				17	4.19 ,,		

Summer time commences at 2 a.m. on 12th April, and ends 2 a.m. on 7th
October.

after sunset. A *green* light, in the case of motor-cars, should be shown in front on the left, and it is compulsory to carry an efficient tail light on the left-hand side to illuminate clearly the back number plates at night time.

Normally the majority of French roads are very good. Cars and motor-cycles entering Paris are stopped, the petrol in the tanks is measured, and *octroi* duty charged.

The roads in Holland are generally good, but narrow and winding. No speed limit is fixed on country roads, but motorists can be charged with driving to the common danger. Some roads are closed to motor traffic.

The general rule of the road in Italy is to keep to the right, but it is frequently reversed in many districts and in many towns.

In Northern Italy and parts of Central Italy, the roads are good and sometimes excellent : in the Southern Provinces the roads are bad.

The speed limit in Spain is 12 kilom. (7¼ miles) per hour.

CHAPTER VIII

FAULTS: THEIR LOCATION AND REMEDY

THE four tables given on succeeding pages afford a convenient method of tracing faults. It requires considerable experience to be able quickly to diagnose the cause of trouble. The beginner must not think from the rather lengthy list that a motor-cycle is always likely to be in trouble. It is only very occasionally that trouble arises.

Some riders have a tendency always to be adjusting and improving the running of the engine. When the engine is running well it is wise to leave it alone.

IGNITION TROUBLES

Testing the Plugs. If it is considered that the engine does not need taking down, yet it is difficult to start, examine the plug, and, holding it by means of the cable (don't hold the plug body with the fingers, for if the plug is defective, a mild but unpleasant shock will speedily make you aware of the fact when the engine is kicked over) so that its metal body touches the cylinder, turn the engine over by means of the kick starter and note whether the spark is regular and "fat." An intermittent spark, or a regular but weak "pin-point" spark, will render starting difficult. It may be that the plug points have become burnt, consequently widening the gap, and in this case the points should be closed. A little gauge for setting the points of the plugs and the contact points of the magneto is on the market; it only costs a few pence, and is well worth having. Failing this, a visiting card may be used as a gauge.

Sooted Plugs. If the plug is sooted or coated with a sticky black film, it should be taken to pieces (plugs with detachable centres are recommended to admit of this) and the centre cleaned with a piece of rag soaked in petrol, and the electrodes (the two points) cleaned bright with a piece of emery cloth. The body of the plug should be scraped out with a knife. The presence of a heavy carbon deposit on the plug shows that the engine is over lubricated, and the remedy here is obvious.

The Gap of the Plug Points. Sometimes, after closing the points of a plug, the rider will notice that the engine requires a different setting of the advance and retard lever to get the same condition of running as was obtained before the plug was adjusted. This is because the closing of the plug points is equivalent to slightly advancing the ignition. The converse is equally true; opening the points will slightly retard the ignition.

Defective Insulation of Plug. Don't forget to inspect the porcelain or mica insulation of the plug, the former may be cracked, and the latter may be " scaling," and a new centre should be purchased if this is found to be the case. (See page 100, which deals with the sparking plug.)

Pre-ignition. Although a plug with scaly mica insulation may appear to be sparking well outside the cylinder, the point to remember is that these " scales " become red-hot and cause pre-ignition, which means the too early firing of the charge. It may be noticed that by advancing the ignition too far a knock is caused, and pre-ignition (see Ignition Troubles) may cause a knock. A little thought will show that if the compressed charge is fired too early the gas is tending to force the piston back before it reaches the top of the stroke. When the spark is ordinarily advanced it actually does this, but beyond a certain limit a knock is heard which ceases when the ignition is retarded. The knock is probably due to the reversal of pressure on the piston head, although there are various theories to account for it. Other causes of pre-ignition are the plug points becoming red-hot, incandescence of carbon deposit or some rough part of the combustion chamber. Do not use plugs with thin electrodes (see also the note on " Pinking " later on).

Defective High-Tension Cable. It is not often that the high-tension cable may cause trouble, but sometimes, if it has been allowed to come into contact with the hot cylinder it may be found that the insulation is burnt away in one spot, allowing the bared wire to touch some part of the engine or other metallic portion and short-circuit the current. To cure this, bind the affected spot with insulating tape. Rain will sometimes cause failure of the ignition or misfiring, due to the water on the cable giving rise to a short circuit. This is comparatively rare.

Trouble with the Contact Breaker. This is not of frequent occurrence, but it must be mentioned. After running the machine for some hundreds of miles it may be found that misfiring develops at high speeds. If the plug is found to be correct, remove the cover of the magneto, rotate the engine by means of the kick-starter, and notice whether the points " make and break," or

FAULTS: THEIR LOCATION AND REMEDY

whether sparking is occurring across them. If the latter is found to be the case, it is almost certain that you will find that the points are pitted and do not make good contact, and they must be carefully trimmed with a file so that the two faces are absolutely flat. If they are not badly burnt, a strip of fine emery cloth may be doubled and pulled backwards and forwards between the points. Incidentally, if the spark across the points is large, the condenser has broken down, and this is a job which can only be put right by the makers. Whilst the cover is off, check the gap by means of the gauge already mentioned, and if incorrect, adjust them with a small spanner until the gauge just passes between them, when they are fully separated by means of the cam.

Broken Contact Spring. If you are riding and the ignition fails suddenly, it is likely that the " make and break " spring has become broken. This means that the points do not return, and quite an effective dodge to get you home is to use a rubber band to return the points.

Rocker Arm Sticking. Sometimes the rider will find that occasional misfiring, or even complete stoppage, is due to the rocker arm in the magneto being stuck. It will be noticed that this has a small bush as a bearing, and in damp weather this sometimes swells and causes the rocker to stick. The proper cure here is to remove the bush and carefully ease it with emery cloth or a file. Do *not* oil it, for even oil will cause the bush to swell.

Defective Carbon Brush. Examine the connection between the carbon brush and the cable. Beads of water or grit may be found between the contacts. It is easy to remove the carbon brush and make quite sure that the carbon is not cracked or broken.

Slipped Magneto Timing. This is caused by the slipping of the sprocket on the armature shaft, of course, causing the spark to occur at the wrong time. To check the timing open the compression tap and pass a piece of wire about 8 in. long through, so that it touches the piston. Now rotate the engine, and by the rise and fall of the piece of wire and watching the valves observe when the piston is at the top of the compression stroke, and then inspect the " make and break " to see that the points are correctly separated.

Testing Twin-cylinder Engines for Misfiring. When irregular running is experienced with a twin-cylinder machine, it is simple to find out which cylinder is misfiring. Obtain a long *wooden* handled screwdriver (you will get a shock if you use a metal handled one) and with the engine running, place the tip of the blade on the plug terminal and touch the cylinder with any other part of the blade ; this will short-circuit the plug so that the engine is only firing on the other cylinder. By testing both cylinders in this way one may soon observe which one is wrong, or whether both are wrong.

Another method is to disconnect the lead from one plug and start the engine, serving the other cylinder in the same way.

CARBURETTOR TROUBLES

Even on the first run the rider speedily becomes aware that the carburettor is a sensitive instrument, which soon complains when it is not correctly adjusted. The levers, he finds, must be set just so for given conditions. Even at best a carburettor is an inefficient device, and a fortune awaits the inventor of one which is truly automatic, supplying the proper mixture for all engine speeds. The writer once made a device which consisted of a sort of chamber in which the gas was mixed, the engine sucking in the properly-mixed gas direct from this chamber. It was quite successful, but too expensive to make.

The rider must learn how to detect inefficient carburation, and so to control the carburettor that an efficient mixture for a given set of conditions is obtained.

The weather has an important effect on carburation. The rider will soon notice that the engine seems to run better at night or in damp weather, and this fact has led many experimenters to try " humidifying " the mixture by injecting water spray into it—with indifferent results up to the present. He will notice that by partly closing the air, opening the throttle, and slightly retarding the ignition, the engine does not seem to knock or thump on steep hills, as it may do even on bottom gear if the adjustment is not made. The author has tried in the succeeding paragraphs to anticipate almost every carburettor trouble, and to show the remedy.

" Popping Back " in the Carburettor. This is one of the commonest carburettor troubles, and usually occurs when the throttle and air are opened beyond a certain point, the effect being occasional popping or " spitting back " through the carburettor—a sort of sneezing of the engine. Gradually closing the air usually will cure it, but if " popping back " in the carburettor occurs when the machine is throttled down to ten or twelve m.p.h., it is a sign that a larger jet is necessary.

FAULTS: THEIR LOCATION AND REMEDY

In changing a jet, it is necessary to see that the fibre washers are removed with the jet, as should one be left at the top of the hole and another jet be fitted, there would be two washers at the top and only one at the bottom, and petrol would leak in consequence. Petrol may leak from the float chamber if the jet is not thoroughly screwed into position, so that this matter should be carefully attended to.

Knocks and "Pinking" Due to Incorrect Mixture. Knocks or "pinking" in engines can be caused through wrong mixture, as well as by mechanical defects or pre-ignition (dealt with later on). Too rich or even too weak a mixture is one of the frequent causes of "pinking," a word which in itself describes the sort of knock given forth. It is an irritating sound like a tap, tap on the inside of the cylinder, and as yet no satisfactory explanation of it has been given. The generally accepted view is that the engine gets very hot owing to the use of too rich a mixture, and at a critical temperature eventually causes the charge to detonate or explode, instead of the flame caused by ignition being slowly propagated. It is, then, *overheating* which really causes "pinking," and it necessarily follows that any cause of overheating also causes pinking.

A jet should be fitted to the carburettor of such a size that full air can just be used at full throttle. A smaller jet is necessary in summer than the one used in winter.

The Petrol Level. Too low a petrol level will cause "popping back," even though the jet be of proper size, but it is wise not to alter the petrol level without good cause. If it is about $\frac{1}{32}$ in. below the top of the jet it is correct, and further adjustment, if necessary, should be made by means of the jet.

Choked Petrol Pipe, etc. Sometimes the petrol pipe will become choked with foreign matter which has found its way through the gauze placed over the tank outlet. In such a case the rider will have mysterious engine stoppages and popping back, due of course to a starved engine. He will stop to inspect, and by that time sufficient petrol has trickled by to enable the carburettor to be flooded, so that the engine starts easily, only to stop again a few yards on. When these symptoms develop, completely disconnect the petrol pipe, and by means of the tyre pump, blow it clean, and also clean out the gauze in the tank and carburettor.

Air Lock. The cause of this trouble has already been fully dealt with, and the rider will be made aware of it by symptoms similar to those already noted in the preceding paragraph. The remedies here given should be applied.

Water in Petrol. This trouble is of a more serious nature, for once water has entered the carburettor it must be taken down and thoroughly wiped dry. It will cause engine stoppage, misfiring, or " popping back." It is wise to drain the tank and use the petrol for cleaning purposes, otherwise the trouble may recur. Also blow the gauzes clear.

Carburettor Flooding. Carburettor flooding is caused by (1) leaning the machine so that the float chamber is raised above the level of the jet (refer back to Fig. 42), (2) grit between the needle valve and the seating, or (3) a float that leaks and has become partly filled with petrol, preventing the needle from seating home. Overheating usually accompanies it, when the flooding takes place whilst riding. The remedy for cause (1) is obvious ; for cause (2) the union connecting the carburettor with the petrol supply should be disconnected and the petrol drained from the carburettor. This will wash the grit away.

A punctured or " petrol logged " float can usually be discovered by noting whether its needle (the " tickler ") is sluggish in action, but if it cannot be so detected, remove the float from the needle and rattle it, when the presence of petrol inside will manifest itself. A piece of sticky paper placed over the hole after the petrol has been shaken out, or even plugging the hole with a piece of soap, will effect a temporary remedy.

Air Leak. This usually takes place between the joints of the induction pipe and carburettor joints, and binding with adhesive rubber tape will speedily cure matters.

Choked Air Vent in Petrol Tank. This is a trouble which the rider may easily mistake for air lock, or choked petrol pipe. It is obvious that as petrol flows from the tank to the carburettor, air must be able to pass into the tank, and if the vent is choked a partial vacuum is formed in the tank, causing air lock. The remedy is obvious.

Damaged Carburettor Slides and Broken Cables. Any trouble with these will present itself in the form of the machine refusing to satisfactorily answer to the operation of the control levers. Sometimes a piece of grit will become lodged between the slides and their barrel, wedging one or both of them, and causing the action to be sluggish. More often than not, however, defective controls are due to frayed or broken cables, and it is wise to get them renewed at the nearest garage ; the job only takes half an hour or so.

If the throttle wire breaks whilst riding, the standard dodge

FAULTS: THEIR LOCATION AND REMEDY

is to change over the air-slide cable to the throttle, and fixing the air-slide in some suitable position, where it is considered it will enable the engine to start easily and run satisfactorily. Don't omit occasionally to oil the cables, by detaching the handle-bar end and letting oil slowly drip between the outer casing and the cable. Stretched cables, a common trouble, should of course be shortened.

TABLE 1
ENGINE REFUSES TO START

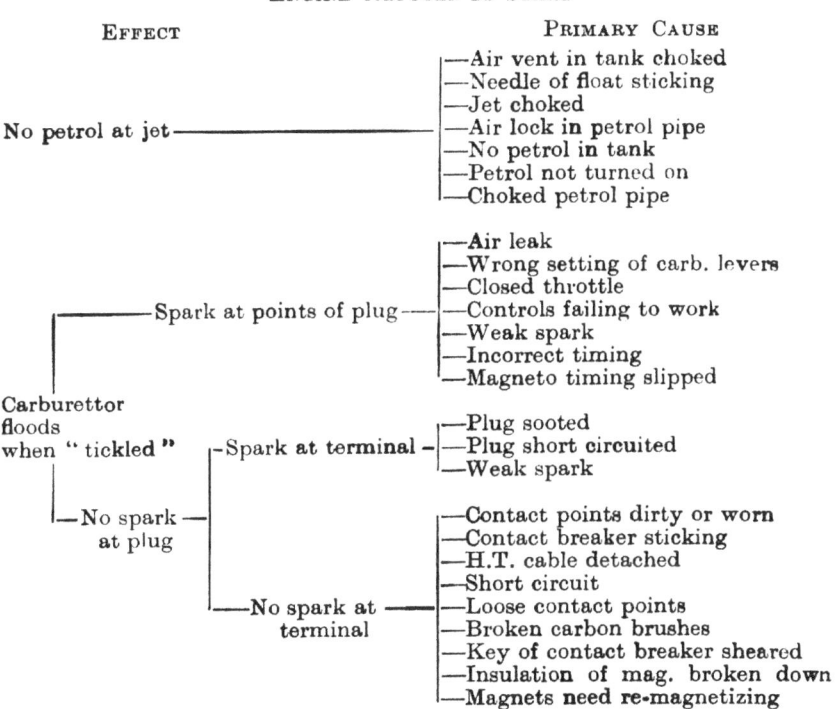

ENGINE TROUBLES

Really the troubles concerned with the engine are caused by one or a combination of the faults dealt with in connection with the carburettor and ignition, but one or two need attention and summary here.

Starting Troubles. One of the chief problems met with in motor-cycling concerns easy starting. When the engine is fairly new and in " tune " it should start from cold without priming, at the first or second kick.

In very cold weather the oil between the piston and cylinder becomes congealed, making it difficult to turn the engine over at an efficient starting speed; also the gas, passing along the cold induction pipe, condenses, so that a proper mixture does not enter the cylinder.

Piston Leakage. This is caused by worn rings, rings gummed up, or uneven cylinder wear. The rings should not be allowed

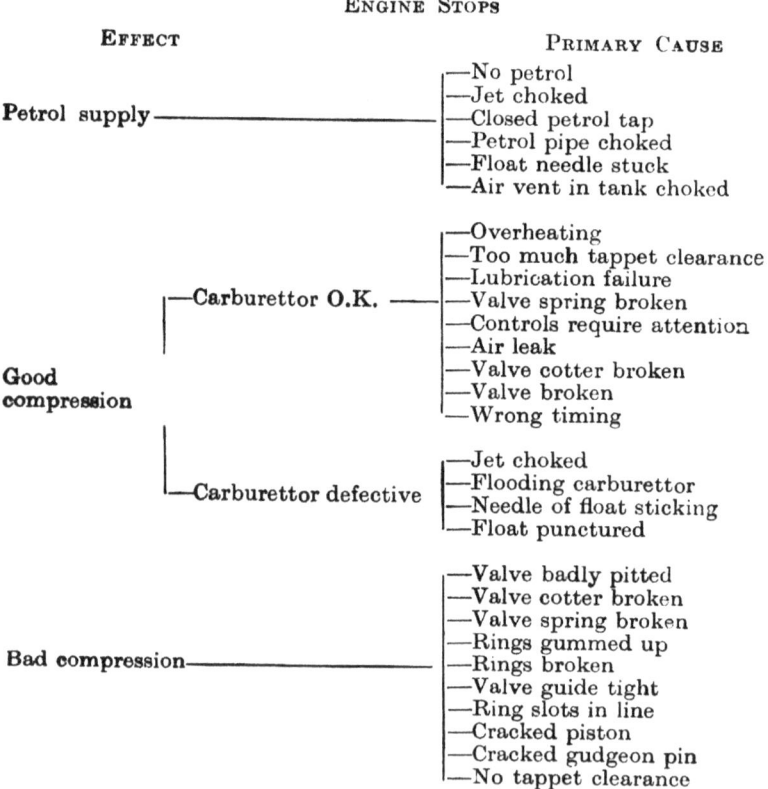

TABLE II
ENGINE STOPS

Effect		Primary Cause
Petrol supply		—No petrol —Jet choked —Closed petrol tap —Petrol pipe choked —Float needle stuck —Air vent in tank choked
Good compression	—Carburettor O.K.	—Overheating —Too much tappet clearance —Lubrication failure —Valve spring broken —Controls require attention —Air leak —Valve cotter broken —Valve broken —Wrong timing
	—Carburettor defective	—Jet choked —Flooding carburettor —Needle of float sticking —Float punctured
Bad compression		—Valve badly pitted —Valve cotter broken —Valve spring broken —Rings gummed up —Rings broken —Valve guide tight —Ring slots in line —Cracked piston —Cracked gudgeon pin —No tappet clearance

to wear so that the gap is wider than $\frac{3}{64}$ in. New rings always leak until they have worn in to the cylinder. Notable loss of power accompanies piston leakage. Where three rings are fitted the gaps should be 120° apart, and when only two are provided 180° apart. When the gaps work into line, slight loss of compression may be noticed.

Leakage Round Plug and Compression Tap. If this is suspected, place some thick oil on the seating, and observe if bubbles form

FAULTS: THEIR LOCATION AND REMEDY

on the compression stroke. A new copper asbestos washer should be fitted if a leak is present.

Broken Valve. A broken valve—which, however, is a very rare occurrence—can be detected by testing the compression, or, presuming the tappets are correctly adjusted, the stem of the broken valve will be in contact with the tappet head.

Valve Bounce. Valve bounce is caused by weak springs, which should at once be replaced.

TABLE III
ENGINE RUNS BADLY

Effect		Primary Cause
Loss of power	Constantly	—Bad compression —Wrong valve clearance —Partial petrol stoppage —Carbon deposit —Bad mixture —Choked silencer —Wrong timing —Cams worn —Gear too high —Weak valve springs
	Intermittently	—Partial petrol stoppage —Controls loose —Valve guide tight
Engine knocks		—Overheating —Excess of air —Ignition too far advanced —Pre-ignition (carbon deposit)
Misfiring	Irregular spark	—Sooted plug —Water in petrol —Contact breaker stuck —Dirty contact points
	Regular spark	—Partial petrol stoppage —Mixture weak —Temporary short circuit

Valve Clearance. Check the valve clearance when the engine is hot, to allow for the expansion. The clearance should be not less than $\frac{1}{64}$ in. An ordinary visiting card is a useful gauge for the purpose.

Valve Sticking. Valve stem may be bent, hole in guide too small, carbon deposit in the guide, or weak spring.

The Cause of "Knocks." Every motor-cycle at some time or other develops what is commonly called "knock." It is a most elusive thing to trace, and, moreover, annoying to the rider.

The knock may not, as we have already seen, always be a mechanical one, but is usually caused by one of the following items: advancing the ignition; too rich a mixture; carbon on the piston getting incandescent and pre-igniting the charge (same effect as too far advance of ignition); loose flywheel (an alarming mechanical knock as if the big ends were loose); play in the big ends or gudgeon pins; magneto sprocket loose on shaft, also cause misfiring.

TABLE IV
ENGINE STOPS DUE TO IGNITION

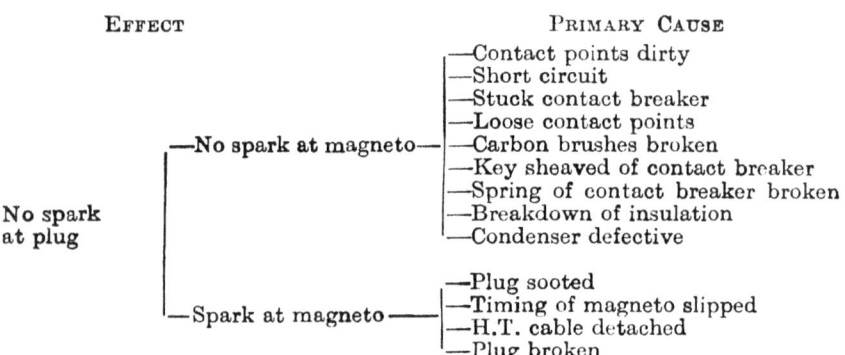

Overheating. Usually due to too rich a mixture, load too heavy, exhaust valve not lifting to full extent, spark retarded, lack of lubrication, excessive use of low gear, gear too high.

Hot Crank Case. Due to worn piston rings or bad compression.

Colour of Exhaust. Black smoke denotes too rich a mixture; blue smoke excess of lubricating oil.

Explosions in Silencer. Due to misfiring or too rich a mixture.

Rapid Deposition of Carbon. Caused by over-lubrication, too rich a mixture, or poor quality of petrol.

CHAPTER IX

LEGAL MATTERS

THE legal matters regarding licensing and registration having been disposed of in Chapter II, it remains to deal with questions anent breakage of the law—what to do and say, and what not to do and say. It is wise to remember that the legal departments of the Automobile Association and the other clubs mentioned, are always glad to advise members who may be involved in difficulties arising out of collisions or other accidents upon the road.

Requests for advice should be made immediately the accident has occurred, and not after the case has been prejudiced by letters having been written or money having been given to other parties involved in the accident.

If representation is desired at the Court, the summons should be sent as soon as served.

What to do in Case of Accident. The first thing to do in case of accident is to obtain the names and addresses of at least two witnesses who are likely to assist your case. Take down on paper careful details of the side of the road on which you were travelling, the speed, the width of the road and the condition of its surface, the signs given (whether by hand or horn, or both), whether the other vehicle (if any) carried lights, and take measurements which may be of assistance to the case, as well as the number of the vehicle and the description. If the owner is wise he will vouchsafe his name and address without cavil, for refusal to do so may be regarded unfavourably. If an injured person is likely to make a claim, an independent medical man should be called to examine him and issue a report. Do not engage in correspondence without legal advice, or if this is not taken, make clear that all your statements in the letter are made without prejudice to your case ; and refrain from making statements, either at the time of the accident or afterwards, which might be construed as an admission of liability. Do not offer money to the injured party, for motives of sympathy may be misconstrued into an admission of legal liability.

The Order to Stop. A person in charge of a horse may order a motor-cyclist to stop, and so may a constable in uniform, or a person injured by your machine. Apart from this, it is inadvisable to stop when asked to do so by others The sign to stop should be made as already noted on page 43.

Endorsement of Licence. A licence cannot be endorsed for the first or second offence of exceeding the speed limit in the parks, nor may it be endorsed when the driver is convicted for obstruction. It may, however, be endorsed for all convictions for offence under the Act, except for first or second offence of exceeding the speed limit. It is not generally known that the holder of a licence which has been endorsed is entitled on renewal or at any time upon payment of 5s. to have a new licence free from endorsements if he has not during a continuous period of not less than three years had any conviction endorsed.

Furious Driving. A person driving furiously renders himself liable to conviction for the following offences—

(1) Driving to common danger.
(2) Exceeding speed limit.
(3) If anyone injured, indictment for causing bodily harm.
(4) If anyone killed, indictment for manslaughter.
(5) To arrest by any person, whether constable or not, who sees offence committed, under the Highway Acts.

Refusing Address. To anyone who complains that the motorist has committed an offence of driving to the common danger, the driver must give his name and address. If the driver refuses, or gives a false name and address, he is liable to fine not exceeding £20 for a first offence, and to heavier penalties for a second or subsequent offence. He may be arrested without warrant by a constable who saw the alleged offence committed, whether the constable is in uniform or not. The owner, if required, must give all the information in his power which may lead to the identification of the driver, and if he does not do so is himself liable to the same penalty as the driver.

Warning of Approach. It is compulsory to give audible warning of approach whenever it is necessary. Failure to do so renders the driver liable to conviction for driving to the common danger, and to an action for negligence if injury is caused as a result of such neglect.

Exhaust Cut-out. It is illegal to use an exhaust cut-out, or any device which enables the exhaust to escape without first passing through the silencer.

Arrest. The driver is liable to arrest by a police constable (whether in uniform or not) if he refuses his name and address, refuses to produce his licence on demand, or if his machine does not bear the identification (registration) mark.

LEGAL MATTERS 131

Illumination. (See also Chapter III.) Motor-cycles with sidecars attached must carry on the latter a white light forward and red light to rear. The driver must have the identification plate illuminated half an hour after sunset and half an hour before sunrise. Solo motor-cycles must also carry a red rear light.

Rules Regarding Number Plate. The driver of a motor-cycle is guilty of an offence if the number plate is not properly fixed, or if it is in any way obscured or rendered not easily distinguishable or not properly illuminated, unless he can prove that he has taken reasonable steps to prevent this, and if the driver is not the owner the latter may be guilty of aiding and abetting.

Regarding the Registration Book. When a licence is issued a Registration Book is handed to the owner, and this must be sent to the Council with whom the vehicle is registered, or
(1) When any alteration is made to the vehicle.
(2) On sale or other change of ownership.
(3) On change of address.
(4) When vehicle broken up, destroyed, or sent permanently out of the United Kingdom (see paragraph in the chapter on " Buying and Selling a Second-hand Machine ").

Obstruction. A motor-cycle must not be left for an unreasonable or unnecessary time on the highway.

Time Limit for Service of Summons. Unless warned at the time the offence is committed, notice of an intended prosecution for exceeding the speed limit must be given to the driver or the registered owner of the motor-cycle within such time after the offence is committed, not exceeding 21 days, as the Court thinks reasonable.

Right of Appeal. A person convicted of any offence under the Motor Car Act, 1903, has the right of appeal to next Court of General Quarter Sessions, provided he did not plead " Guilty," in Courts other than Metropolitan. A right of appeal lies against an order disqualifying any person from obtaining a driver's licence.

Speed Limit. According to the strict letter of the law, the speed must not exceed 20 miles per hour on the highway. Special limits of 8 or 10 miles per hour are fixed in certain towns and villages. These must be strictly observed.

CHAPTER X

BUYING AND SELLING AN OLD MOUNT

Buying a Second-hand Machine. The purchase of a second-hand machine is one which should be carefully approached by the inexperienced, for so many machines with serious engine troubles which outwardly appear to be in excellent condition are available that it is difficult to detect fakes, especially when skilfully executed. Only the most reputable makes should be purchased, for one may then be reasonably assured of being able to obtain spares. A skilled motor-cyclist where possible should accompany the inexperienced. The very efficient B.S.A. spares service enables spare parts for any particular B.S.A. model, however old, to be obtained within a few hours. It is always wise to purchase a second-hand machine from a reputable agent.

Year of Make. First ascertain the year of make (this may be verified by reference to the registration book) by noting the engine and frame numbers. A list of engine and frame numbers of B.S.A. machines from 1914 onwards can be obtained from the manufacturers.

Examining the Machine. First examine the frame for cracks, and to see that it is true. Next look to the condition of the tools and accessories, and test the head and front forks for play. The tyres and wheel bearings should not be missed, and the points of attachment need viewing if a sidecar is fitted. Having satisfied oneself that in general the machine is in reasonable condition, proceed to test the engine. The condition of the nuts is a good index as to whether the machine has needed frequent adjustment.

Testing the Engine. Firstly, turn the engine over slowly by means of the kick-starter and see that the compression is good. Next rotate it and listen for knocks indicative of wear. Perhaps greatest wear will be detected in the valves and valve gear, but these parts are easily and cheaply replaced. If the valves have been repeatedly ground in this fact will readily be apparent (refer back to Fig. 83), for the valve seats will be relatively wide and deep sunk, and is an index of careless use or old age—a fact which should temper one's views of the other parts. The valve-gear mechanism should be exposed and the wheels and cams carefully examined. If worn they will require renewal.

BUYING AND SELLING AN OLD MOUNT

The condition of the piston and cylinder can only be gauged by experience, but if wear is detected (piston will " slap " in the cylinder when the engine is running) an allowance might be asked. It must be pointed out that a piston which slaps in its cylinder should not be regarded as a minor defect—it usually is indicative of an oval cylinder, necessitating regrinding of the cylinder and a new (oversize) piston, and it is wise not to make a purchase. There is an exception in the case of an alloy piston. This is a fairly loose fit in the cylinder when cold.

The Trial Run. After the preliminary inspection, the engine should be started and attention devoted to noise caused by worn cams and timing gears, worn piston or cylinder, or other engine noises. A trial run should in all cases be insisted on, so that one may be satisfied as to the control and general running. The trial run can easily be arranged with a combination, for the owner, if dubious, can accompany the prospective purchaser in the sidecar. If a solo machine, the owner can reasonably expect a deposit as a token of good faith before allowing the intending purchaser to take a trial run. If satisfied that the machine is in good condition, bargain for a reduction in price, for most owners ask for more than they expect to get for the machine. Second-hand prices may be ascertained by reference to the weekly motor-cycle papers.

A Warning. The reader is advised to make quite sure that the vendor is the real owner of the machine, for if he purchases and the machine is subsequently claimed by the real owner, he must return the machine to the rightful owner and has no redress except the doubtful one of suing the vendor if he can be found. Carefully inspect the registration book and check the name and address.

Selling a Second-hand Mount. The foregoing information indicates in some measure the questions likely to be asked, and before taking steps to dispose of the machine it should be placed in reasonable selling condition. As such it will avoid irritating correspondence after sale, and will command a higher price than if the defects are left unremedied ; as well, excuses have not to be raised when the defects are discovered by the purchaser.

Selling Through an Agency. Several firms undertake to sell second-hand machines, the procedure in most cases being to value the machine and to allow the agent a commission on that price. As, however, such agents usually sell the machine at a higher price than the owner's figure, it follows that too high a value renders the machine of little service to the agent.

Part Exchange. When the purchase of a new machine is contemplated, best value for the old one can be obtained by a part exchange transaction.

Selling by Advertising in Trade Papers. This is usually an excellent method of selling, because the trade papers classify the machines, so that an intending purchaser of a B.S.A. has only to look down the small advertisement columns of one of the motor cycling papers to see comparative prices. The fact cannot be ignored that a prospective purchaser of a second-hand machine buys either *The Motor Cycle*, or *The Motor Cyclist Review*, and this method of selling is recommended.

Advertising in the daily and local press is also an excellent method of selling.

The reader is reminded of the rules given in Chapter III (regarding the registration book) which apply when the machine changes hands. Post Card Form No. R.F. 70 must be filled in and posted by the vendor of a second-hand motor-cycle. It is obtainable at all post offices. Do not let the machine change hands until the purchase price is handed over.

Checking the Age of a Second-hand Machine. If an intending purchaser is in doubt as to the exact age of a machine, he can check it by means of the engine and frame numbers. These cannot, however, be taken as an absolutely definite guide; they are simply works numbers.

The reader will readily appreciate that if there is no material change in design in a certain model from one season to another, that model ceases to belong in particular to the expired season, and since the maker's guarantee dates from the sale of the machine by the agent to the customer, and not its delivery from the works, frame and engine numbers are a rough guide only; they are, however, essential for identification when ordering replacements of any description.

CHAPTER XI

USEFUL INFORMATION

TABLE OF GRADIENTS

Gradient.	Per Cent.	No. of Feet Rise or Fall in 1 Mile.
1 in 5	20	1,056
1 ,, 6	17	880
1 ,, 7	14	754
1 ,, 8	$12\frac{1}{2}$	660
1 ,, 9	11	587
1 ,, 10	10	528
1 ,, 11	9	480
1 ,, 12	8	440
1 ,, 13	$7\frac{3}{4}$	406
1 ,, 14	7	377
1 ,, 15	$6\frac{1}{2}$	352
1 ,, 16	$6\frac{1}{4}$	330
1 ,, 17	6	311
1 ,, 18	$5\frac{1}{2}$	293
1 ,, 19	5	278
1 ,, 20	5	264
1 ,, 25	4	211
1 ,, 30	3·3	176
1 ,, 35	2·8	154
1 ,, 40	$2\frac{1}{2}$	132

EQUIVALENT SPEEDS

Speed in M.P.H.	Time Taken to Cover 1 Mile.
10	6 minutes
15	4 ,,
20	3 ,,
25	2 ,, 24 seconds
30	2 ,,
35	1 minute $42\frac{6}{7}$,,
40	1 ,, 30 ,,
50	1 ,, 12 ,,
60	1 ,,

APPROXIMATE ENGINE REVOLUTIONS
At Different Speeds — Miles per Hour

Gear Ratio.	4	4¼	4½	4¾	5	5¼	5½	5¾	6	6¼	6½	6¾	7
Speed in Miles Hour.													
5	260	276	292	309	325	346	358	374	388	404	420	437	453
10	520	552	584	618	650	692	716	748	775	808	840	875	905
15	780	828	876	927	975	1038	1074	1122	1160	1210	1260	1310	1360
20	1040	1104	1168	1236	1300	1384	1432	1496	1550	1615	1680	1750	1810
25	1300	1380	1460	1545	1625	1730	1790	1870	1940	2020	2100	2180	2265
30	1560	1656	1752	1854	1950	2076	2148	2244	2320	2420	2520	2620	2720
35	1820	1932	2044	2163	2275	2422	2506	2618	2710	2830	2950	3060	3170
40	2080	2208	2336	2472	2600	2708	2864	2992	3100	3230	3370	3490	3620
45	2340	2484	2628	2781	2925	3114	3222	3366	3490	3640	3790	3940	4070
50	2600	2760	2920	3090	3250	3460	3580	3740	3880	4040	4310	4370	4530
55	2860	3036	3212	3399	3575	3806	3938	4114	4270	4440	4680	4800	4980
60	3120	3312	3504	3709	3900	4152	4296	4488	4650	4850	5040	5240	5440

Diameter of Driving Wheels, 26 in. For 28 in. Wheels, multiply by 0·93.
For 24 in. Wheels, multiply revolutions by 1·08.

USEFUL INFORMATION

CYLINDER BORES AND STROKES IN MILLIMETRES AND INCHES

An Approximate Guide for Comparison

A Cylinder Measuring—		Is Equal to—
Millimetres		Inches
60 × 61½	=	2¾ × 2$\frac{7}{16}$
63 × 80	=	2½ × 3⅛
72 × 85½	=	2$\frac{13}{16}$ × 3⅜
76 × 85	=	3 × 3$\frac{5}{16}$
80 × 98	=	3⅛ × 3⅞
85 × 98	=	3$\frac{5}{16}$ × 3⅞
90 × 90	=	3$\frac{9}{16}$ × 3$\frac{9}{16}$
90 × 110	=	3$\frac{9}{16}$ × 4$\frac{5}{16}$
95 × 115	=	3¾ × 4$\frac{9}{16}$
100 × 115	=	3$\frac{15}{16}$ × 4$\frac{9}{16}$
105 × 118	=	4⅛ × 4⅝
108 × 120	=	4¼ × 4¾
110 × 125	=	4$\frac{5}{16}$ × 4$\frac{15}{16}$
112 × 128	=	4$\frac{7}{16}$ × 5$\frac{1}{16}$
114 × 130	=	4½ × 5⅛
116 × 134	=	4$\frac{9}{16}$ × 5$\frac{5}{16}$
118 × 138	=	4⅝ × 5$\frac{7}{16}$
120 × 140	=	4¾ × 5½
122 × 143	=	4$\frac{13}{16}$ × 5⅝
124 × 146	=	4⅞ × 5¾
126 × 148	=	4$\frac{15}{16}$ × 5$\frac{13}{16}$
128 × 150	=	5$\frac{1}{16}$ × 5$\frac{15}{16}$

FORMULAE FOR H.P.

S = Stroke in centimetres
D = Diameter of cylinder in centimetres
R = Revolutions per minute
N = Number of cylinders

R.A.C. Formula H.P. $= \dfrac{D^2 \times N}{16 \cdot 13}$

A.C.U. Formula = 100 c.c. = 1 h.p.

A more accurate formula is the Dendy Marshall in which—

$$\text{H.P.} = \dfrac{D^2 \times S \times N \times R}{200,000}$$

TYRE SIZE EQUIVALENTS

65 Millimetres	= 2½ in.		650 Millimetres	= 26 in.	
80 ,,	= 3 ,,		700 ,,	= 28 ,,	
85 ,,	= 3¼ ,,		750 ,,	= 30 ,,	
90 ,,	= 3½ ,,		800 ,,	= 32 ,,	
100 ,,	= 4 ,,		870 ,,	= 34 ,,	
105 ,,	= 4¼ ,,		910 ,,	= 36 ,,	
120 ,,	= 5 ,,		1010 ,,	= 40 ,,	

LIST OF B.S.A. SPARE PART STOCKISTS

Town.	Name of Stockist.	Address.
Aberdeen	J. Dawson	39 Thistle Street
,,	D. C. Cruickshank	347 Union Street
Aldershot	Phillips Bros.	Birchett Road and Cranmore Lane
Banbury	Trinder & Osborne	2 & 3 Broad Street
Barnstaple	Arch. Jones	70 High Street
Bedford	Imperial Cycle Co.	58 St. Loyes
Belfast	W. J. Chambers	106 Donegall Pass
Berwick-on-Tweed	Lion Garages, Ltd.	Lion Garage
Birkenhead	H. J. Marston	50 Argyle Street
Birmingham	County Cycle & Motor Co., Ltd.	301 Broad Street
(Aston)	Falcon Cycle & Motor Depot (E. Newell)	54 Lozells Road
(Edgbaston)	Cranmore Bros.	5 Upper Hagley Road
(Hay Mills)	H. Bird & Sons	1045 Coventry Road
(Rubery)	Owen's Garage	New Road
(Small Heath)	J. J. Woodgate	Small Heath Park Motor and Cycle Depot
(Sparkhill)	A. Watkins	550 & 565 Stratford Road
Blackpool	J. Hall	143 Church Street
Bournemouth	S. Priestley	35 Seamoor Road
,,	Knott Bros.	214-8 Charminster Road
Bradford	C. Sidney, Ltd.	140-2 Manningham Lane
Bridgend	J. Lewis	35 Caroline Street
Bridgwater	Anderson & Wall	18 St Mary Street
Brighton	Bradshaw's	6 Western Road, Hove
Bristol	S. J. Fair	201 Cheltenham Road
Burnley	Wilde & Co.	181 St. James' Street
Bury	Arthur Coyle	33 Walmersley Road
Cambridge	King & Harper	6 and 7 Bridge Street
Canterbury	G. R. Barrett & Son	30 St. Peter's Street
Cardiff	J. Parsons & Co.	2 Albany Road, Roath Park
Carlisle	W. T. Tiffen	Irishgate Brow
Carmarthen	W. Edwards & Sons	Towy Garage
Chapel-en-le-Frith	Lomas Bros.	Newfield Garage
Chatham	H. G. Russell	Fountain Garage, High Street
Chelmsford	H. T. Hadler	New Street
Cheltenham	Leslie Paynter	Bath Street
Chester	Davies Bros.	34 Bridge Street
Chesterfield	M. Brooks	Holywell Street
Colchester	The Motor Cycle and Light Car Depot	119 High Street
Coventry	Coventry Motor Mart, Ltd.	London Road
Croydon (West)	Godfreys, Ltd.	228-234 London Road
Darlington	Duplex Motor & Cycle Co.	8-12 & 23 Grange Road
Derby	Campion Cycle Co.	59 & 61 London Road
,,	Kay & Scampton	14 Sadlergate

USEFUL INFORMATION 139

LIST OF B.S.A. SPARE PART STOCKISTS—(contd.)

Town.	Name of Stockist.	Address.
Doncaster	W. E. Clark & Co.	27 & 29 Station Road
Dorchester	Tilley's	31 South Street
Eastbourne	F. Ray & Sons, Ltd.	47 Seaside Road
,,	Bradshaw's	10 Terminus Road
East Grinstead	Fosters (East Grinstead) Ltd.	79 London Road
Edinburgh	Alexander & Co.	113-115 Lothian Road
Evesham	Frank Morrall, Ltd.	Central Garage, 20 Port St.
Exeter	Wessex Garage Co.	60 Longbrook Street
Frome	P. Difazio	25 Catherine Street
Gateshead	O. Carmichael & Son	81-83 High West Street
Glasgow	Bell Bros.	223 St. George's Road
,,	Alexander & Co.	272-274 Great Western Road
,,	Rossleigh, Ltd.	532 Great Western Road
,,	Hamilton Bros.	Buchanan Street
Gloucester	Boakes & Harper	1 Worcester Street
Goldthorpe (Yorks.)	A. Wigfield	Furlong Road
Gravesend	Barty's Motor Works	Central Garage
Grimsby	J. Plastow & Son	13 & 15 Osborne Street
Guildford	J. E. Jackson	97 High Street
Halifax	Halifax Motor Exchange	25 Horton Street
Hampton-in Arden	J. Pearson	Barston
Harrogate	H. Acklam	Strawberry Dale
Hastings	F. Ray & Sons, Ltd.	29-30 Havelock Road
Hawick	Milligan & Bell	7 Bridge Street
Haywards Heath	J. W. Dinnage	Sussex Road
Hereford	A. Kear & Co.	52b Commercial Street
Hitchin	J Chalkley & Son	Brand Street
Horsham	Jackson Bros.	London Road
Huddersfield	Earnshaw	10 Cloth Hall Street
Hull	A. E. Brown	47½-48 Witham
Inverness	Alex. Munro	14 Falcon Square
Ipswich	Revett's	Barrack Corner Garage
King's Lynn	The "Sandringham" Cycle Works (Messrs. J. Cox & Sons)	Railway Road
Kingston-on-Thames	H. Taylor & Co., Ltd.	135 London Road
Kirkcaldy	Wm. Christie	11 Whytescauseway
Launceston	J. Wooldridge & Son	Western Road
Leeds	J. Armitage & Sons	York Street
,,	Watson, Cairns & Co., Ltd.	Lower Briggate
Leicester	E. W. Campion & Sons	Welford Place
Lincoln	West's (Lincoln) Ltd.	115c High Street
Liverpool	Campion Cycle Co.	70 Renshaw Street
,,	Cundle's	24 Old Haymarket
,,	J. Edwards & Sons	452-462 Rice Lane, Walton
London, N.W.1	Godfrey's, Ltd.	366-368 Euston Road
,, N.7	J. Grose, Ltd.	255-257 Holloway Road
,, E.C 2	J. Grose, Ltd.	4 Old Jewry, Cheapside
,, S.E.6	F. Parks & Son	5 & 6 Central Parade, Catford
,, W.C.1	Referee Cycle, Co., Ltd.	332 High Holborn
,, W.12	Turner's Stores	180-2 Railway Approach, Shepherd's Bush

LIST OF B.S.A. SPARE PART STOCKISTS—(contd.)

Town.	Name of Stockist.	Address.
London, E.7	Lovett's, Ltd.	418 Romford Road, Forest Gate
,, S.E.18	Cleare & Co.	125 Woolwich High Street
,, S.W.11	Owen Bros.	19 Battersea Rise, Clapham Common
,, (Twickenham)	C. A. Blay	192 Heath Road
Lowestoft	Taylor Bros.	75 London Road
Luton	F. H. Moss	Park Street
Maidstone	Anstey & Son	30-34 Stone Street
Manchester	W. H. Jones	415 Bury New Road, Higher Broughton
,,	Colmore Depot	209 Deansgate
,,	Tom Davies	229 Deansgate
,,	Stretford Garage	1073 Chester Road, Stretford
Middlesbrough	Pallister, Yare & Cobb, Ltd.	134 Marton Road
Nelson	Wilde & Co.	95 and 97 Manchester Road
Newcastle-on-Tyne	Kirsop, Murray & Co., Ltd.	12 Hood Street
,,	Dene Motor Co.	Haymarket
Newmarket	H. W. Kelty & Son	High Street
Newport (Mon.)	V. T. Waite	79 Commercial Street
Northampton	P. C. Spokes	1 Henry Street
Norton (Malton, Yorks.)	Bower's Motor Exchange	Church Street
Norwich	H. Chapman	42 Duke Street
Nottingham	E. W. Campion & Sons	Station Street
Oxford	Laytons of Oxford	New Road
Perth	M. Shaw & Sons	22 Mill Street, and 137-143 High Street
Peterborough	Burrows Bros.	57 Westgate
Peterhead	J. Campbell & Sons	34½-38 St. Peter Street
Plymouth	A. E. Snell (Mrs.)	97 Old Town Street
Portsmouth	Suitalls	250-258 Commercial Road
Preston	Loxham's Garages Ltd.	Charnley Street, Fishergate
Pulborough (Sussex)	Gray & Rowsell	Burygate
Reading	Fortescue Bros. Ltd.	1 and 2 West Street
Redhill	The Redhill Motor and Cycle Works	50 Brighton Road
Rhyl	Nelson's	39 Queen Street
Rotherham	Walter Wragg	27 Effingham Street
St. Austell	S. H. Kellaway & Sons	South Street Garage
Salisbury	W. Rowland & Sons	86-106 Castle Street
Sheffield	Walter Wragg	Wellington Street
Sherborne	Sheppards Garage (Sherborne) Ltd.	South Street
Shetland	Thomson's Garage	Esplanade, Lerwick
Shrewsbury	J. C. Pickering	49 Mardol Road, and Smithfield Road
Southampton	B. B. Tebbutt	54 Commercial Road
Southport	H. F. Brockbank	58 Lord Street
Southsea	Percy Kiln, Ltd.	Elm Gove
Stockton-on-Tees	Stan Jones	Bridge Road

LIST OF B.S.A. SPARE PART STOCKISTS—(contd.)

Town.	Name of Stockist.	Address.
Stoke-on-Trent	J. & N. Bassett	Howard Place, Shelton
Stratford-on-Avon	A Bolland & Co.	Guild Street
Sunderland	Dunn & Jameson	100-106, Hylton Road
Sutton-in-Ashfield	W. Henstock	29-43 Forest Street
Swadlincote	T. H. Wroughton	High Street Garage
Swindon	J. Easter & Sons	8-10 King Street
Taplow	H. E. West	Bath Road
Taunton	W. P. Edwards	58 East Street
Thetford	W. & G. Lambert Ltd.	Cycle and Motor Works
Tonbridge	Chas. Baker & Co.	150 High Street
Tunbridge Wells	G. E. Tunbridge	2 Vale Road
Warsop	E. Poynton	Central Garage, Market Place
Watford	Lloyd, Cooper & Co.	61 Queen's Road
Wednesfield	Wednesfield Motor and Cycle Garage	Wolverhampton Road
Wellingborough	H. V. Briggs, Ltd.	High Street
Westcliffe-on-Sea	J. Costin & Son	237 London Road, Southend
Weymouth	Tilley's	The Esplanade
Winchester	Winchester Cycle and Motor Co.	Jewry Street
Windsor	S. A. Surplice	37 and 39 Sheet Street
Workington	J. Wilkinson	43 Washington Street
Worthing	F. Wheatland	56 Broadwater Street (West)
Yarm-on-Tees	T. B. Dobson & Sons	High Street
Yeovil	The Yeovil Motor Mart	Hendford
York	C. S. Russell	32 Lawrence Street

VELOCEPRESS BOOKS & MANUALS

VELOCEPRESS MANUALS - MOTORCYCLE

1930'S BRITISH MOTORCYCLE CARBS & ELEC COMPONENTS (BOOK OF)
1930'S BRITISH MOTORCYCLE ENGINES (OVERHAUL & MAINTENANCE)
1930'S BRITISH MOTORCYCLE GEARBOXES & CLUTCHES (BOOK OF)
AJS 1932-1948 SINGLES & TWINS 250cc THRU 1000cc (BOOK OF)
AJS 1945-1960 SINGLES 350cc & 500cc MODELS 16 & 18 (BOOK OF)
AJS 1955-1965 SINGLES 350cc & 500cc (BOOK OF)
ARIEL UP TO 1932 (BOOK OF)
ARIEL 1932-1939 PREWAR MODELS (BOOK OF)
ARIEL 1933-1951 (WORKSHOP MANUAL)
ARIEL 1939-1960 4 STROKE SINGLES (BOOK OF)
ARIEL 1958-1964 LEADER & ARROW (BOOK OF)
BMW R26 R27 (1956-1967) FACTORY WORKSHOP MANUAL
BMW R50 R50S R60 R69S (1955-1969) FACTORY WORKSHOP MANUAL
BRIDGESTONE 90 SERIES FACTORY WSM & PARTS CATALOGUE
BRIDGESTONE 175 SERIES FACTORY WSM & PARTS CATALOGUE
BSA BANTAM ALL MODELS FROM 1948 ONWARDS (BOOK OF)
BSA SINGLES & V-TWINS UP TO 1927 (BOOK OF)
BSA SINGLES & V-TWINS UP TO 1930 (BOOK OF)
BSA SINGLES & V-TWINS UP TO 1935 (BOOK OF)
BSA SINGLES & V-TWINS 1936-1939 (BOOK OF)
BSA OHV & SV SINGLES 250-600cc 1945-1959 (BOOK OF)
BSA OHV & SV SINGLES 250cc 1954-1970 (BOOK OF)
BSA OHV SINGLES 350 & 500cc 1955-1967 (BOOK OF)
BSA TWINS 1948-1962 (BOOK OF)
BSA TWINS 1962-1969 (SECOND BOOK OF)
CYCLEMOTOR (BOOK OF)
DOUGLAS 1929-1939 PREWAR ALL MODELS (BOOK OF)
DOUGLAS 1948-1957 POSTWAR ALL MODELS FACTORY SHOP MANUAL
DUCATI 160cc, 250cc & 350cc OHC MODELS FACTORY SHOP MANUAL
HONDA 50 ALL MODELS UP TO 1970 INC MONKEY & TRAIL (BOOK OF)
HONDA 90 ALL MODELS UP TO 1966 (BOOK OF)
HONDA 125-150cc TWINS C/CS/CB/CA FACTORY WORKSHOP MANUAL
HONDA 250-305 TWINS C/CS/CB FACTORY WORKSHOP MANUAL
HONDA C100 SUPER CUB FACTORY WORKSHOP MANUAL
HONDA C110 SPORT CUB 1962-1969 FACTORY WORKSHOP MANUAL
HONDA TWINS & SINGLES 50cc THRU 305cc 1960-1966 (BOOK OF)
HONDA TWINS ALL MODELS 125cc THRU 450cc UP TO 1968 (BOOK OF)
J.A.P. ENGINES 1927-1952 & MOTORCYCLES 1934-1952 (BOOK OF)
LAMBRETTA 1947-1957 ALL 125 & 150cc MODELS (BOOK OF)
LAMBRETTA 1957-1970 LI & TV MODELS (SECOND BOOK OF)
MATCHLESS 1931-1939 ALL MODELS 250cc THRU 990cc (BOOK OF)
MATCHLESS 1945-1956 350 & 500cc SINGLES (BOOK OF)
MATCHLESS 1955-1966 350 & 500cc SINGLES (BOOK OF)
NEW IMPERIAL ALL SV & OHV FROM 1935 ONWARDS (BOOK OF)
NORTON 1932-1939 PREWAR MODELS (BOOK OF)
NORTON 1932-1947 (BOOK OF)
NORTON 1938-1956 (BOOK OF)
NORTON 1955-1963 MODELS 19, 50 & ES2 (BOOK OF)
NORTON 1955-1965 DOMINATOR TWINS (BOOK OF)
NORTON 1957-1970 TWINS FACTORY WORKSHOP MANUAL
NSU PRIMA 1956-1964 ALL MODELS (BOOK OF)
NSU QUICKLY 1953-1963 ALL MODELS (BOOK OF)
PANTHER 1932-1958 LIGHTWEIGHT MODELS 250 & 350cc (BOOK OF)
PANTHER 1938-1966 HEAVYWEIGHT MODELS 600 & 650cc (BOOK OF)
RALEIGH MOPEDS 1960-1969 (BOOK OF)
RALEIGH MOTORCYCLES 1919-1933 (BOOK OF)
ROYAL ENFIELD 1934-1946 SINGLES & V TWINS (BOOK OF)
ROYAL ENFIELD 1937-1953 SINGLES & V TWINS (BOOK OF)
ROYAL ENFIELD 1946-1962 SINGLES (BOOK OF)
ROYAL ENFIELD 1958-1966 250cc & 350cc SINGLES (SECOND BOOK OF)
ROYAL ENFIELD 736cc INTERCEPTOR FACTORY WORKSHOP MANUAL
RUDGE 1933-1939 (BOOK OF)
SUNBEAM 1928-1939 (BOOK OF)
SUNBEAM 1946-1957 S7 & S8 (BOOK OF)
SUZUKI 50cc & 80cc UP TO 1966 (BOOK OF)
SUZUKI T10 1963-1967 FACTORY WORKSHOP MANUAL
SUZUKI T20 & T200 1965-1969 FACTORY WORKSHOP MANUAL
TRIUMPH 1935-1939 PREWAR MODELS (BOOK OF)
TRIUMPH 1935-1949 (BOOK OF)
TRIUMPH 1937-1951 (WORKSHOP MANUAL)
TRIUMPH 1945-1955 FACTORY WORKSHOP MANUAL
TRIUMPH 1945-1958 TWINS (BOOK OF)
TRIUMPH 1956-1969 TWINS (BOOK OF)
VELOCETTE 1925-1970 ALL SINGLES & TWINS (BOOK OF)
VESPA 1951-1961 (BOOK OF)
VESPA 1955-1963 125 & 150cc & GS MODELS (SECOND BOOK OF)
VESPA 1955-1968 GS & SS (BOOK OF)
VESPA 1963-1972 90, 125 & 150cc (THIRD BOOK OF)
VILLIERS ENGINE UP TO 1959 INC. 3 WHEELERS (BOOK OF)
VILLIERS ENGINE UP TO 1969 (BOOK OF)
VINCENT 1935-1955 (WORKSHOP MANUAL)

VELOCEPRESS TECHNICAL BOOKS – MOTORCYCLE

CATALOG OF BRITISH MOTORCYCLES (1951 MODELS)
INDIAN PONYBIKE, BOY RACER & PAPOOSE ILL PARTS LIST & SALES LIT
MOTORCYCLE ENGINEERING (P.E. Irving)
SPEED AND HOW TO OBTAIN IT (Motor Cycle Magazine UK)
TUNING FOR SPEED (P.E. Irving)

VELOCEPRESS MANUALS - THREE WHEELER'S

BSA THREE WHEELER (BOOK OF)
VINTAGE MORGAN THREE WHEELER (BOOK OF)

VELOCEPRESS MANUALS - AUTOMOBILE

ALFA ROMEO GIULIA WORKSHOP MANUAL 1300 TO 2000cc 1962-1975
ALFA ROMEO GIULIA TECH MANUAL CARBURETED CARS FROM 1962
ALFA ROMEO GIULIA TECH MANUAL FUEL INJECTED CARS FROM 1969
AUSTIN-HEALEY 6-CYLINDER WORKSHOP MANUAL
AUSTIN-HEALEY SPRITE & MG MIDGET WORKSHOP MANUAL 1958-1971
BMW 600 LIMOUSINE FACTORY WORKSHOP MANUAL
BMW 600 LIMOUSINE OWNERS HAND BOOK & SERVICE MANUAL
BMW 2000 & 2002 1966-1976 WORKSHOP MANUAL
BMW ISETTA FACTORY WORKSHOP MANUAL
CORVAIR 1960-1969 WORKSHOP MANUAL
CORVETTE V8 1955-1962 WORKSHOP MANUAL
FIAT 500 FACTORY WORKSHOP MANUAL 1957-1973
FIAT 600, 600D & MULTIPLA FACTORY WORKSHOP MANUAL 1955-1969
JAGUAR E-TYPE 3.8 & 4.2 SERIES 1 & 2 WORKSHOP MANUAL
JAGUAR MK 7, 8, 9 & XK120, 140, 150 WORKSHOP MANUAL 1948-1961
METROPOLITAN FACTORY WORKSHOP MANUAL
MGA & MGB OWNERS HANDBOOK & WORKSHOP MANUAL
MG MIDGET TC, TD, TF & TF1500 WORKSHOP MANUAL
PORSCHE 356 1948-1965 WORKSHOP MANUAL
PORSCHE 911 2.0, 2.2, 2.4 LITRE 1964-1973
PORSCHE 912 WORKSHOP MANUAL
TRIUMPH TR2, TR3, TR4 1953-1965 WORKSHOP MANUAL
VOLKSWAGEN TRANSPORTER, TRUCKS & WAGONS 1950-1979 WSM
VOLVO 1944-1968 ALL MODELS WORKSHOP MANUAL

VELOCEPRESS TECHNICAL BOOKS - AUTOMOBILE

FERRARI 250/GT SERVICE AND MAINTENANCE
FERRARI GUIDE TO PERFORMANCE
FERRARI OWNER'S HANDBOOK
FERRARI TUNING TIPS & MAINTENANCE TECHNIQUES
HOW TO BUILD A FIBERGLASS CAR
HOW TO BUILD A RACING CAR
HOW TO RESTORE THE MODEL 'A' FORD
MASERATI OWNER'S HANDBOOK
OBERT'S FIAT GUIDE
PERFORMANCE TUNING THE SUNBEAM TIGER
SOUPING THE VOLKSWAGEN
SOLEX CARBURETORS (EMPHASIS ON UK & EU AUTOMOBILES)
SU CARBURETORS (EMPHASIS ON UK AUTOMOBILES)
WEBER CARBURETORS (EMPHASIS ON ALFA & FIAT)

VELOCEPRESS BOOKS & GUIDES - AUTOMOBILE

ABARTH BUYERS GUIDE
COMPLETE CATALOG OF JAPANESE MOTOR VEHICLES
FERRARI 308 SERIES BUYER'S AND OWNER'S GUIDE
FERRARI BERLINETTA LUSSO
FERRARI BROCHURES AND SALES LITERATURE 1946-1967
FERRARI BROCHURES AND SALES LITERATURE 1968-1989
FERRARI OPP, MAINTENANCE & SERVICE H/BOOKS 1948-1963
FERRARI SERIAL NUMBERS PART I - ODD NUMBERS TO 21399
FERRARI SERIAL NUMBERS PART II - EVEN NUMBERS TO 1050
FERRARI SPYDER CALIFORNIA
HENRY'S FABULOUS MODEL "A" FORD
MASERATI BROCHURES AND SALES LITERATURE

VELOCEPRESS BOOKS – RACING

CARRERA PANAMERICANA - MEXICAN ROAD RACE (BOOK OF)
DIALED IN - THE JAN OPPERMAN STORY
IF HEMINGWAY HAD WRITTEN A RACING NOVEL
VEDA ORR'S NEW REVISED HOT ROD PICTORIAL

AUTOBOOKS WORKSHOP MANUALS & BROOKLANDS ROAD TEST PORTFOLIOS

FOR A COMPLETE LISTING OF THE AUTOBOOKS & BROOKLANDS TITLES THAT WE CURRENTLY HAVE AVAILABLE, PLEASE VISIT OUR WEBSITE.

FOR A DETAILED DESCRIPTION OF ANY OF THE TITLES LISTED ABOVE PLEASE VISIT OUR WEBSITE AT:
www.VelocePress.com

INDEX

A

Abroad, taking machine, 116
Acceleration, 33
Accident, what to do in case of, 129
Address, refusing, 130
Advance and retard, object of, 57
Advance, use of, 34
Advertising second-hand machine, 132
Air leaks, 124
—— lock, 123
—— vent, choked, 124
Aligning sidecar, 108
Aluminium piston, 67
Animals, unattended, on road, 44
Appeal, right of, 131
Approach, warning of, 130
Arrest, 130
Auto-Cycle Union, 26
Automobile Association and Motor Union, 26

B

Brake adjustments, 34, 104
——, engine as, 38
Brakes, 88
——, adjusting, 34
——, oil on, 35
——, use of, 34
Braking on hills, 38
——, jab, 35
B.S.A. stockists, 138
Buying second-hand machine, 132

C

Cable, high-tension, defective, 120
Cables, broken, 124
Camber of road, 44
Cam-cush drive, 65
Caps, 114
Carbon brush, defective, 121
——, rapid deposition of, 128
Carbon, removing from engine, 97
——, " popping back " in, 122
——, principle of, 53
—— slides, damaged, 124
—— troubles, 122
Chain, front driving, adjusting, 101
——, magneto, adjusting, 100
——, rear, adjusting, 102
Chains, care of, 101
Cleaning the machine, 106
Club, joining, 26
Clubs—
  Autocycle Union, 26
  Automobile Association and Motor Union, 26
  Royal Automobile Club, 26
Clutch, 71
—— adjustments, 105
——, dog, of three-speed gear, 68
——, operating, 31
——, parts, 72, 73
——, slipping, 33
Coasting, 33
Combination outfit, driving 36
——, making left-hand turn with, 36
Contact breaker, trouble with, 120
—— spring, broken, 121
Continental touring, 116
Controls, action of, 31
——, engine, 29
Corner, how to take, 42
—— sign, 41
Corners and cross roads, 41
Countershaft gear, two-speed, 66
Courtesy, 45
Crankcase, cleaning out, 98
——, hot, 128
Cross roads and corners, 41
Cush drive, 64
—— ——, cam-faced, 65
—— ——, purpose of, 64
Cylinder bores, equivalent, 137

143

D

Dangerous corner sign, 40
Decarbonizing engine, 97
Disc adjusting hub, 86
Dog clutch, of three-speed gear, 68
Dress, choice of, 112
Drip feed, adjusting, 29
Drive, cam cush, 65
——, cush, 65
Driving, furious, 130
—— in traffic, 42
—— licence, 20

E

Enamelling, 110
Engine as brake 38
—— controls, 29
——, decarbonizing, 97
——, elements of, 49
——, how it works, 49
——, lubricating, 29
——, misfiring, twin cylinder, 121
——, petrol supply to, 30
——, priming, 31
——, procedure after starting, 31
——, re-assembling, 99
—— revolution, table of, 136
——, running after assembly, 99
——, starting, 30, 31
—— stops, 126
——, strokes of, 48
—— troubles, 125–128
——, types of, 47
Exhaust, colour of, 128
——, cut-out, use of, 130
Exhaust-valve lifter, 33
—— ——, timing, 99

F

Faults, locating, 119
Flywheel, function of, 49
Fork spring, 107
Forks, adjusting and lubricating, 106
Four-stroke engine, elements of, 49
—— ——, principle of, 49

G

Gear changing, 31, 71
—— for starting, 31

Gear, timing, 82, 87
——, two-speed countershaft, 66
——, operating, 31
Gradients, table of, 135
Grease-gun lubrication, 91
Guides, 115

H

Hand signalling, 40
Hats, 114
Headwear, 114
Helmets, 114
High-tension cable, defective, 120
Hill, braking on, 38
——, starting down, 38
——, starting on, 37
——, stopping on, 37
Horns, law regarding, 26
Horse-power, calculating, 137
Horses, led, 43

I

Ignition, timing, 100
—— troubles, 128
Illumination, law regarding, 131
Inlet valve, timing, 99
Insurance, 27
International travelling passes, 116

J

Jab braking, 35
Jet, level of petrol at, 56
Joints, making, 107
——, making washers for, 109

K

Knocks, 123
——, cause of, 127

L

Lamps, 25
Leakage, piston, 126
—— plug and compression tap, 126
Left, turning to, 40
Legal matters, 129
Level of petrol, adjusting, 56
Licence, driving, 20
——, endorsement of, 130
Lighting-up time table, 117
Lubricating the engine, 29

INDEX

Lubrication details, 33
——, grease-gun, 91
—— system, 74

M

Magneto, adjusting, 100
—— advance and retard, 34
—— chain, adjusting, 100
—— contact breaker, trouble with, 120
—— —— spring broken, 121
—— rocker arm sticking, 121
——, timing, 100
—— timing, slipped, 121
Make-and-break, action of, 51
Maps, 115
Mixture, incorrect, 123

N

Night riding, 45
Number plate, rules regarding, 131
—— plates, 24, 52

O

Obstruction, 131
—— on the brakes, 35
Overhauling, 92
Overheating, 128
Overtaking other vehicles, 46

P

Paper washers, making, 109
Periodicals, 134
—— level, 56
—— pipe, air-lock in, 123
—— ——, choked, 125
—— pipes, coiling, 109
—— supply to, 30
—— tank ; choked air vent, 124
——, water in, 124
Pillion riding, 37
Pinking, 123
Pipe joints, 107
——, petrol, choked, 125
——, ——, how to coil, 109
Piston, aluminium, 67
—— leakage, 126
—— ring gaps, position of, 98
—— rings, examining, 98
—— rings, removing, 98

Plate clutch, 73
Plug, defective insulation, 120
—— points, adjusting, 120
——, sooted, 119
——, sparking, cleaning, 100
Pocketed valves, 100
Pottering, 43
Pre-ignition, 120
Premiums, insurance, 27
Priming the engine, 31
Pump, auxiliary, 34

R

Rear light regulations, 25
Re-enamelling, 110
Registration, 22
—— book, 131
Retard and advance, object of, 57
——, use of, 34
Right, turning to, 42
Rings, piston, removing and examining, 98
Risks, insuring against, 27
Road, camber of, 44
—— prohibited sign, 41
——, proper side of, 41
——, rules of, 38
—— signs, 41
——, unattended animals on, 44
Roads, cross, 42
Rocker arm sticking, 121
Royal Automobile Club, 26
Rules of road, 38
—— ——, continental, 117

S

Second-hand mount, buying, 132
—— ——, selling, 133
" Seizing " : what it is, 29
Selling machine, 133
Shock absorber, 90
Sidecar, aligning, 108   [36
—— alignment, effect on tyres,
—— outfit driving, 36
—— outfit, making left-hand turn with, 36
Side-valve engine explained, 47
Sign, dangerous corner, 41
——, " Road Prohibited," 41
——, R.A.C., 41
——, speed limit, 41

INDEX

Signs, road, 41
Silencer, explosions in, 128
—— : why used, 83
Skids and tramlines, 43
Sooted plugs, 119
Spare part stockists, 138
Spares : what to carry, 115
Sparking plug, cleaning, 100
—— ——, defective insulation, 120
—— —— points, adjusting, 119
—— ——, sooted, 119
Speed limit, 41, 131
—— —— sign, 41
Speeds, equivalent, 135
Spring forks, adjusting and lubricating, 106
—— of forks, removing, 107
Starting troubles, 125
Steering and sidecar alignment, 36
—— head, adjusting and oiling, 107
Stockists, B.S.A., 138
Stop, order to, 129
Stopping, 34
—— in traffic, 42
——, warning of, 43
Studs, tight, removing, 110
Summons, time limit for service, 131

T

Tables—
 Cylinder bores and strokes, 137
 Engine refuses to start, 125
 —— runs badly, 127
 —— stops, 126
 —— stops due to ignition, 128
 —— revolutions, 136
 Formulae for h.p., 137
 Gradients, 135
 Lighting-up times, 117
 Speeds, equivalent, 135
 Tyre size equivalents, 137
Tanks, filling, 29
Tappet clearance, adjusting, 92
—— ——, testing, 92

Tax, 20
Three-speed countershaft gear, 67
Time-table, lighting up, 117
Timing gear, 82
—— magneto, slipped, 121
—— the magneto, 100
—— the valves, 99
Tour, planning, 116
Touring, 112
Traffic blocks, negotiating, 43
——, driving in, 42
——, passing other, 43
—— pottering, 43
——, stopping in, 42
—— rules, modifying, 45
Tram, driving behind, 44
Tramcars, passing, 43
Tramlines and skids, 43
Turning to right or left, 40
Two-speed countershaft gear, 66
Two-stroke principle, 57
—— sizes, equivalent, 137
Tyres and sidecar alignment, 36
——, " hard," 35
——, pressure of, 36
——, pressure of, correct, 37
——, " soft," 37

V

Valve, broken, 127
—— bounce, 127
—— clearance, 127
—— sticking, 127
Valve timing, 87
——, pocketed, 100

W

Washers, paper, making, 109
Water in petrol, 124
Wellingtons, 112
—— spin, 33
—— truing, 109
Windscreens, 115

www.ingramcontent.com/pod-product-compliance
Lightning Source LLC
Chambersburg PA
CBHW070331170420
43201CB00012B/1807